INDIANS

INDIANS

THE GREAT PHOTOGRAPHS THAT REVEAL

NORTH AMERICAN INDIAN LIFE, 1847-1929, FROM THE UNIQUE

COLLECTION OF THE SMITHSONIAN INSTITUTION

by JOANNA COHAN SCHERER

with JEAN BURTON WALKER

BONANZA BOOKS
New York

Editor-in-Chief: Jerry Mason
Editor: Adolph Suehsdorf
Art Director: Albert Squillace
Associate Editor: Moira Duggan
Associate Editor: Barbara Hoffbeck
Art Associate: Mark Liebergall
Art Associate: David Namias
Art Production: Doris Mullane

For Andy Gage

Frontispiece:
Kicking Bear, a Dakota (Miniconjou Band).
Inspired by Wovoka, the Paiute prophet, he brought the
Ghost Dance religion to the Dakota in 1890.
William Dinwiddie/Bureau of American Ethnology,
Washington, D.C./1896.

For the Cohans who taught me persistence and the Scherers who showed me much patience

CONTENTS

PREFACE

2631. PUEBLO LAGUNA, N.M.

This book grew out of an exhibit of Indian photographs selected from the Smithsonian Institution National Anthropological Archives. The exhibit, entitled *Indian Images: Photographs of North American Indians, 1847-1928,* opened at the Smithsonian Festival of American Folklife during the summer of 1970 and has been traveling since.

Many people have contributed information on the photographs and I wish to acknowledge their help. They are: Christian Feest, Keith Basso, Sidney Brinckerhoff, Robert Euler, Bill Holm, Frederica de Laguna, Catharine McClellan, Alfonso Ortiz, Peter Stone, Wayne Suttles, Jack Williams, and Muriel Wright. In addition, a number of Smithsonian associates have given their time and advice to aid this project. They include: Raymond DeMallie, Anne Morgan, Jo Moore, Richard Smart, William Sturtevant, and John Wooten. To all I express my thanks. A special note of thanks must go to Jean Burton Walker, who made this a book.

The photographs in this book cover the brief period in North American Indian history from 1847 to 1929. The year 1847 is the date of the first photographs in the Smithsonian collection; by the year 1929 the impact of white European-Americans on red men had been so overwhelming that it is difficult to see, in photographs taken after that date, any vestige of how the Indians lived before their encounter with white culture.

The pictures here, aided by a brief text, are intended to show the reader the tremendous changes that took place in Indian life during those eighty-two years, with a view to understanding a little more fully what men were like when they were an integral part of the earth. Because the camera has the unique ability to reveal as much of times gone by as it does of the moment, one can glimpse the Indian's proud past.

The first chapter contains portraits that show the immense variety in the appearance of North American tribes. The second chapter shows how tribes of different geographical regions lived: what their houses were like, how they obtained their food, how they lived off their land, and how they worshipped their universe. The third section is a selection of Indian envoys who came to Washington, D.C., to get treaties with the United States Government fulfilled and to reclaim the lands the Government had expropriated. The geographical areas portrayed are: the Great Plains, the Southwest, the Great Basin, California, the Northwest Coast, the Arctic, the Subarctic, the Southeast, and the Northeast. A map on page 190 shows the location of each tribe represented in this book at the time of contact with white men.

Wherever possible in the captions, Indians are identified by name, whether their own or that given them by whites. The name of the person's tribe is given first and followed, where known, by the name of the band to which he belonged in parentheses. The number given each photograph by the Bureau of American Ethnology is listed in the back of the book.

J. C. S.

Many pioneer photographers, such as Jackson on left, took pictures of Indians as they followed the frontier across the Nation. Not only did a photographer have to transport his camera, but also his darkroom, tripod, chemicals, dishes, measurers, pails, and often his own water. In all equipment could weigh up to two hundred pounds.

William Henry Jackson/Laguna Pueblo, New Mexico/1870s (Courtesy Robert Weinstein)

THEY LOOKED

The image of the North American Indian has been widely exaggerated by fanciful tales of trappers, explorers, settlers, writers, and movie directors. Two myths, equally unrealistic, have flourished. The first, circulated by European travelers under the influence of Rousseau's romanticism, idealized the Indian as the perfect child of nature, blissfully unaware of the discords of civilization. The second regarded him as the last vestige of primitive savagery, the spawn of hell, ever ready to plunder and murder.

Neither was true. Each was merely an image focused in the newcomer's eye. Religious, social, and economic preconceptions of the white man's place in the universe impeded the first adventurers and settlers from understanding or recording fully the richness of Indian culture.

No one knows, or probably ever will know, exactly how the first Americans lived before the Europeans arrived. They left no written record and early archaeological evidence is scarce. That part of their history, however, covers at least twelve thousand years—from the migrations across the Bering land bridge, during the last Ice Age, until explorers set foot on Indian land in 1492. From a letter of Columbus we do know that they were "men of great deference and kindness."

At that time there were approximately three hundred different tribes in North America speaking perhaps as many as five hundred different languages. The poetic richness of each language was a mirror to nature, reflecting the beauties and characteristics of a particular tribe's region, whether mountains or plains, cedar or sage, showers or snows, buffalo or deer.

They were called Indians because Columbus thought he had discovered a new route to India. Most tribes called themselves by the animal they knew themselves to be—the human beings. The pseudonym Indian was the first misconception created by Europeans.

In a brief three hundred years, from an early battle against the colonists at Pequot Fort in 1637 to their massacre at Wounded Knee in 1890, they were compelled to give up much of their way of life. And with that went their lands, customs, dress, and homes. By 1890 most of the tribes had been forced onto reservations throughout the West and, by their absence, made way for miners, cattlemen, sheepherders, and farmers.

The daguerreotype was invented in 1839, the camera ten years later, and together they made manifest the destiny of the Nation. Photography caught the young country in the midst of its westward drive and, at the same time, captured aboriginal Indian culture in the twilight of its days. By recording the ascendancy of the white men, it preserved the last glimmer of the old ways of the Indians.

The year 1847, the date of the first picture in this collection, marks the midpoint of the Nation's expansion from the Mississippi River to the Pacific Coast. It was a time of transformation for the country from an agrarian to a technological society. In addition, it was the beginning of the floodtide of European immigration. Whereas one million settlers came to the New World between 1800 and 1840, five and a half million arrived in the two following decades.

The products and inventions of the industrial revolution required new lands and resources and, simultaneously, made territorial expansion feasible. The United States annexed Texas in 1845, and in 1846 settled the boundary of the Oregon Territory—what is now Washington, Oregon, and Idaho—through a compromise treaty with England. Two years later the

Preceding pages: CROW
L to r: Sees the Ground, Pretty
Paint, Comes Up Red,
and Victor Singer lined up for
a foot race in 1910.

Richard Throssel/Bureau of Reclamation.

12

young Nation defeated Mexico and acquired all the remaining territory west of the Rio Grande, above the Gila River, to the Pacific. By 1848 everything that was to be the mainland of the United States was secured except for the Gadsden Purchase, a small strip acquired in 1853.

Between the end of the Civil War and the massacre of Big Foot's band at Wounded Knee, industrialization accelerated the pace of Manifest Destiny. And in those twenty-five years the battalions of progress proved to be redoubtable foes of the Indians.

Railroads were the greatest boon to the stampeding of the West and dealt an iron blow to the tribes. The link-up of the Central Pacific and Union Pacific in 1869 completed the first of four transcontinental lines built through Indian lands—all of them in violation of Thomas Jefferson's promises, made sixty years before, that the plains west of the Mississippi would remain Indian.

By 1890 the country was covered by 150,000 miles of iron rails and wooden ties. The iron horse brought in settlers, miners, agents, missionaries, buffalo hunters, and farmers. Relentless in its tracks, it carried the Indians away from their ancestral homelands to Federal reservations.

Although the railroads brought about the end of the aboriginal Indian culture, the reports of their routes have, ironically, preserved much information about the traditional ways of the red men.

Each railroad exploration had its official photographer. The Government was interested not only in terrain and watercourses, but also wanted to know what Indians future travelers might encounter. The photographers took many pictures of different tribes to fill the survey reports, but the cameras rarely caught purely aboriginal dress. Instead they recorded inroads already made by foreign trappers and traders, some twenty to forty years earlier.

The first photographer to accompany a railroad expedition was John Mix Stanley. He went as the official artist on Isaac I. Stevens' 1853 journey to establish a northern rail route to Washington, which was not yet a state. The proposed tracks were to go through the heart of Blackfoot country and Stanley painted and daguerreotyped tribesmen along the way. The camera impressed the Indians mightily though, unfortunately, none of the photographs survived. Stevens, the survey leader, reported in his account to the 36th Congress that, "Mr. Stanley commenced taking daguerreotypes of the Indians with his apparatus. They were delighted and astonished to see their likeness produced by direct action of the sun. They worship the sun, and they considered Mr. Stanley was inspired by their divinity, and he thus became in their eyes a great medicine man."

The 1870s marked a new era in Government exploration. Gone were the days of railroad surveys. The country had been crossed. The new decade was filled with scientific expeditions sent to discover what the land had to offer both to eastern business interests and to future settlers.

Ferdinand Vandiveer Hayden was among those commissioned by the Government to collect and describe the minerals and natural resources of the West. William Henry Jackson, considered by many to be one of the greatest American photographers, joined the 1871 expedition to Yellowstone. Hayden, whom the Indians appropriately called Man-Who-Picks-Up-Stones-Running, and Jackson explored the northern Plains, the Yellowstone River, and the land of the Crow.

The United States had acquired the Great Plains as part of the $15 million Louisiana Purchase in 1803 from France. 13

During the years between the Purchase and Jackson's arrival with his camera the influence of trappers and troopers was great. Trappers—the singular mountainmen—were the first to see the land's extent and the first to exploit its riches, and troopers—the Army's cavalrymen—were the agency of the Government's implacable policies that recognized the rights of whites to settle and railroads to run, but not of Indians to stay where and as they were.

Material goods quickly made their way into the Plains culture and by the time Jackson began to photograph the Crow, many were wearing factory-made shirts, city-styled hats, and peace medals awarded by the Government to important Indians promising their allegiance.

Until the nineteenth century, the Indians of the Great Plains made most of their clothing from the hides of antelope, deer, sheep, elk, and buffalo. More than any other regional group, the Plains Indians had to adapt to vast extremes of climate. The summers were oppressively hot and the winds of winter icy cold. Following the vagaries of temperature, the men sported buffalo-skin breechclouts in summer and in winter wrapped themselves in warm but cumbersome buffalo robes. A buffalo killed in winter afforded the greatest warmth, and a hide with its heavy winter coat could weigh up to ninety pounds.

For hundreds of years the great buffalo furnished the Plains Indians with hides for clothes and tepees, meat for pemmican, sinew for bows, and horns for cups. The 1870s, however, ended all that. Professional hide-hunters arrived with their powerful buffalo rifles, and by 1883 they had decimated an estimated thirty million head. With the passing of the bison, the Indians were forced to give themselves up to reservation life and adopt the clothing and accouterments of white men. Government blankets took the place of the mighty buffalo robes, and baggy trousers replaced the scant breechclouts.

In earlier times, the hallmark of the Plains clothing style had been quillwork. Canada porcupines then lived in the cottonwood trees along the rivers of the northern prairies and were hunted for both their quills and their flesh. The quills were pulled from the hide and stored in pouches made from buffalo bladders. They were used to adorn just about everything: tunics, headbands, cradleboards, tobacco bags, and pipestems.

Glass beadwork, now so familiar, began to take the place of quillwork in the 1800s. Mountainmen and traders, in search of beaver pelts, reached the Rockies in the 1780s and traded with the Indians the little brightly colored glass beads—in addition to whiskey and gunpowder—for the soft furs.

Because fashion changed in the 1830s and Europe tired of the fur felt hat made from beaver pelt, the beaver trade dwindled. But the demand for beads among the Plains Indians continued. Beadwork was much easier to apply and soon took the place of quillwork. By the time the camera made its way west, the old art had nearly died out. But some old chiefs wore their venerable shirts for special occasions, such as having their pictures taken.

The United States gained what is now California, Nevada, Utah, New Mexico, Arizona, and western Colorado in 1848. The territorial acquisition settled the war with Mexico and added more than a half million square miles to the Nation. The topography was dazzling, the ground rich in minerals, and many of the Indians peaceful. By the seventies it had become a favorite site for geologists and anthropologists.

The first river exploration of the area was conducted by Major John Wesley Powell in 1868, when he journeyed down the Colorado into the chasms of what he called the Great Unknown. John K. Hillers, who later became the official photographer for the Bureau of American Ethnology, accompanied Powell on his second Colorado River Expedition in 1871. Hillers, a tenderfoot, had been picked up in Salt Lake City as an oarsman. After two professional photographers left the group, Hillers became the cameraman for the expedition and took many pictures of the Ute, Paiute, Zuni, and Hopi.

When Powell and Hillers explored the desert regions of the Great Basin on the west bank of the Colorado, they found the Paiute, a nomadic tribe, undergoing rapid change. Some were dressed as they had been for several hundred years. They either went naked or wore robes of rabbit fur and flimsy cloth made from the fibers of the milkweed. On the east bank of the Colorado, in what is today considered the Southwest, they found Hopi and Zuni living in pueblos of stone and mud and wearing clothes of wool and cotton.

When the Spaniards conquered the people of the Southwest in the 1500s, they introduced sheep and some techniques of spinning and weaving wool. Until their arrival, almost all clothes were made of cotton, which was grown in damp streambeds and the washes of rivers. However, it was an unalterable fact of life that the success of the cotton crop was marginal.

Sheep were well suited to the hot, dry climate and the Indians quickly adopted herding and wove blankets and many of their clothes from wool. Despite its popularity, cotton continued to be used by several tribes for ceremonial occasions. The Hopi, a tribe to the north of the Little Colorado River, wore cotton when they married. A young suitor would weave a white robe for his bride, which she wore at their wedding and in which she was shrouded after death.

What is known today as Navajo weaving was also practiced by both Zuni and Hopi, and the term has become generic for all weaving in the Southwest. The art is notable for the careful use of pleasing colors. Before the introduction of modern dyes, urine was an essential element in fixing the colors and, perhaps, the secret of their clarity. Green was made from the leaves of the *Yucca baccata*, blue from charred wood several months buried in the ground, white from clay, and black from charcoal. Whether for blanket or saddle girth, the looms were the exact size of the cloth to be woven, and the material was never cut.

Although the Indians of the Southwest have adopted many European styles, they still make some of their own cotton and woolen fabrics. Weaving is practiced on reservations and, through sales to tourists, provides one of their means of income.

Although far to the north, the myriad islands along the coast of Canada are warmed by the Japan Current. The winters are mild and the land protected from the cold by heavy mist and fog. The rivers teem with salmon and grayling, the woods are filled with deer and elk, and the cool, damp climate and rich soil give rise to giant cedars.

Alexander Mackenzie, a stalwart man among mountainmen, was the first trapper to reach the Northwest by an overland route. He went there in 1793 in search of

15

beaver on behalf of the British Northwest Company, which later merged with Hudson's Bay Company. The warm, striped blanket, the latter's trademark, traded for pelts, came to wrap many an Indian and is often apparent in photographs of the northwestern coastal people.

Meriwether Lewis and William Clark were the first overland Americans to meet coastal Indians. The explorers arrived at the mouth of the Columbia River, the southern limit of the Northwest Coast region, in November, 1805. From their journals we know that the people made their clothes from the innerbarks of evergreens, which they frayed, twined, tied, and wove into thick shirts, pants, shoes, and cloaks.

By far the most beautiful creation wrought from bark was the Chilkat blanket of the Tlingit, a tribe far up the coast. The blanket was a splendid ceremonial robe worn only on important occasions. One of the more ornate of all woven fabrics, it was made on the simplest of looms. The loom consisted merely of two forked poles set into the ground, across which a warp pole was placed. This was the entire structure. The vertical warp strands were made from finely shredded cedar bark intertwined with spun hair of the white Rocky Mountain goat. Bladder bags covered the loose strands at their lower end to keep them clean and, when the blanket was finished, the ends formed a long, luxurious fringe.

Equally important, however, was the spinning and dying of the white goat hair prior to the weaving. Hemlock bark mixed with urine stained the spun strands black, lichens colored them yellow, and a mixture of copper alloys dyed them blue. Then nimble fingers wove the weft of dyed goat hair into the warp without even the aid of a hand heddle to push the strands tightly into place. The careful juxtaposition of colors determined intricate patterns. Similar designs are found on ceremonial masks, totem poles, houses, and boats along the coast.

Alaska was purchased in 1867 from Russia for the meager sum of $7,200,000. Only after gold was discovered in the 1880s did explorers go into the interior, usually starting from the mouth of either the Laird or the Yukon. The Government sent an Army mission to explore the river in 1883, and much of the early information we have on how the Alaskan Eskimos lived comes from its official accounts. Some of the earliest photographs of the Eskimos in this collection were taken by E. W. Nelson, who accompanied a meteorological expedition sponsored by the Alaska Commercial Company, which ran a steamer on the Yukon.

Ethnologists believe the Eskimos to be direct descendants of people who crossed the Bering land bridge from Siberia long after the ancestors of the North American Indian. The survival of the Eskimos has been the result of ingeniousness. They have managed to exist for thousands of years in the face of what would seem insurmountable odds—a scarcity of wood for fire, for instance, and vegetation for food.

The chief concern of the Eskimos was to keep warm and dry against the chilling winter winds and icy snows. They wore several layers of clothing, largely the skins of caribou, which they hunted inland in summer. Furs were warmer but difficult to come by. A hunter could wait on the frozen offshore waters of the Arctic Ocean for countless hours and never-ending northern days to spear a seven-foot Alaska fur seal when it came up for air.

A whale-intestine parka was essential. It was tough, durable, and waterproof.

Sometimes walrus or seal was used instead, but a whale was by far the most glorious of catches. The intestine of a fifty-foot bowhead, harpooned in early summer when the ice broke, could clothe many families.

Bird feathers were favored for warm and beautiful jackets. Both the common eider duck and the double-crested cormorant were frequently used. The eider duck is found in the Arctic during the summer months and has a wonderfully soft plumage that allows no seepage. As the eider preens itself, it constantly replenishes its coat with an oily, waterproof secretion. The breast feathers of the female are as downy and warm as their namesake—eiderdown. The shiny greenish-black feathers of the cormorant are not so waterproof, but they do retain body heat.

Photographers had no opportunity to record the original clothes or customs of the eastern Indians. By the time the daguerreotype was invented in 1839, the Iroquois and Algonquian tribes in the North had been confined to reservations. In the South, most of the Five Civilized Tribes—Creek, Seminole, Cherokee, Chickasaw, and Choctaw—had been banished from their homelands to the Indian Territory west of the Mississippi. Their exodus, ordered by an act of Congress, began in 1832 and took ten years. The Cherokee exodus is known as the Trail of Tears because about a quarter of the people that began the trek westward perished. The Indians who managed to survive tried to reestablish the pattern of existence they had known in the Southeast. In the second half of the century scholars such as James Mooney of the Bureau of American Ethnology studied and photographed descendents of the few Cherokees who refused to go and who remained in their native North Carolina by hiding in the mountains. They are known today as the Eastern Cherokee.

Most of our knowledge of how the Indians in the East looked comes from sixteenth- and seventeenth-century chroniclers and artists. Eastern Indians made their clothing primarily from the skins of the abundant whitetail deer and from the plentiful grasses and the innerbarks of elm and cedar. In fact, the southern tribes twined bark so finely that Spaniards in the 1500s often mistook the weave for cotton.

Awls were commonly used for sewing by the eastern tribes until metal needles were introduced by Europeans in the 1600s. They were carefully carved from the leg bones of deer or turkey. The instrument was sharpened to such a keen point that it required its own special case, often made of a hollowed thigh bone or cane.

With the utmost care, the skins were sewn together with deer or buffalo sinew. (Buffalo roamed the East until the eighteenth century.) The sinew came from the long tendon stretching down either side of the spine. First the tendons were hung out, then slender strands were peeled off for thread as needed. For extra strength, they were frequently twisted or plaited together.

Just as the metal needle replaced the delicate awl, so the sewing machine replaced the needle. Invented in 1846, it quickly made its way into the manufacture of Indian clothes. The Seminoles who refused to leave their homes in Florida to go to the Indian Territory adopted some European fashions. Flounces and ruffles took the place of fringes, and fancy ribbons replaced nuts and milk-teeth bands on skirts and sleeves. The yoked bodice came into vogue in the United States in the 1880s and is seen in many photographs taken at the turn of the century.

Just as photographers of the 1850s and sixties were interested in how the Indians looked, the ethnologist-photographers of the seventies and eighties were interested in peculiarities of dress and style. The customs of paint and tattooing, the symbolism of hairdos, and the skills involved in making jewelry were all studied with tremendous curiosity, written up in monographs, and compiled in many publications of the Bureau of American Ethnology.

Tattooing was a prevalent custom among several North American tribes, from the Catawba in the South to the Haida on the Northwest Coast. Men and women alike were fond of it and considered the indelible ornaments to be marks of beauty. Most tribes used tattoos to decorate the flesh while some, such as the Chippewa of Canada, used the process as a form of acupuncture to cure toothaches. In the Southeast, tattooing died out in the late 1700s, but in some parts of Alaska it was practiced into the twentieth century to mark a young girl ready for marriage.

From the diaries and drawings of early explorers we know that many Cherokee and Creek pricked ornate swirls, dots, and bands all over their bodies. They used either fine flint points or brittle pine needles to make little holes in their skin. Black soot from burning pine was rubbed into the raw flesh so that when the punctures healed a series of black dots remained. Sometimes tattoos were applied at puberty, and the occasion was one of great ceremony.

Paint was considered by most tribes to be a powerful agent. It guarded against the glare of the sun and snow, and warded off evil spirits. The designs were highly personal and associated with a man's spirit. Some Mandan painted two hands on their chest if they seized an enemy. Women of some southwestern tribes wore their face paint all the time, and several pictures by William Dinwiddie show them with their markings.

The colors were both easy to apply and simple to remove. Spit and grease were the essential ingredients. Some tribes, such as the Zuni of the Southwest, mixed the paint directly in their mouths and then spat it upon their bodies. Others, like the Northwest Coast Indians, were more fastidious and greased their skin first and then applied dried colored powder.

Red was the color of strength and success to some of the Plains Indians, and it was also the color designating the East, whence all help from the spirits came. The Bloods, a band of the Blackfoot, were so-called from their practice of painting their faces with the red earth of their land, which once extended from the Columbia plateau to the Red River. They also used yellow from the gallstones of buffalo and black from burned aspen branches.

White was the color symbolizing the East among the peace-loving people of the Southwest. Among the Hopi, whose name means "Peaceful Ones," it was the color of the cotton bridal gowns and of the squash blossom—their symbol of fertility. Seri women used white clay and colored pigments on their cheekbones to designate their family relationships. These insignia went from mother to daughter and could be worn only by women.

Each color had its own little sac for safekeeping. Because he had no pockets, an Indian was continually in need of pouches. They were the custodians of his dyes, his elk teeth, nut beads, bird feathers, porcupine quills, and clam-shell hair pincers. The vital pouches were made from the bladder, stomach, or membrane surrounding the heart of elk, deer, or buffalo.

When the last of the Indians were

confined to reservations, paint began to lose its importance in Indian culture. Warriors no longer wore it to defend their homelands, and it did not protect them from going to work in the lumber mills of Minnesota or the power plants of New York.

A body without hair was a thing of beauty to many Indian tribes. Both men and women had naturally very little, and the sparse beard of the men was generally plucked out with salt- or fresh-water clam shells. The Pawnee, of the central Plains, pulled out even their eyebrows.

More important was the dressing of hair. Customs and fashions differed from tribe to tribe. Loose and flowing tresses were the style among the Nez Perce of the Columbia plateau, and plaits with a red-painted part was the custom among the Dakota. Sometimes the latter added false braids of black horse hair, and to smell especially delicious they laced their locks with sweetgrass and the seeds of columbine.

Besides plucking out their beards and eyebrows, Pawnee men also shaved the sides of their heads, leaving only the top ridge and crown scalplock. This they dressed with a pomade of charcoal and grease to keep the hair stiff and standing straight. The style was also worn by the neighboring Oto and Osage and some northeastern tribes. The cut has been memorialized by some schoolboys who, even today, sport what they proudly call "Mohawks."

There were haircuts for children, adolescents, brides, and mourners. A child's first haircut was accompanied by much ceremony, because it was integrally associated with his life and spirit. The Omaha cut a boy's hair into the shape of his protective animal, whether turtle or bear. When a young Hopi maiden reached puberty her hair was first washed with the ground root of yucca and then twirled into a large swirl above each ear to symbolize the blossoms of the fertile squash, which the tribe cultivated in abundance. Once she married, she dismantled the whorls and wore her hair in two simple plaits, or bound bunches, down her back.

Hair was often believed to be the link between the people and the spirits. Families in mourning often cut off their hair, and widows frequently sheared it around their ears. The bereaved of some tribes, such as the Salish of the Northwest, hung their tresses on the eastern branches of the red-fir trees.

Scalping is the most renowned link between hair and death. It is not known exactly who started the practice, but it has been well established that early on the British offered a bounty of forty pounds for an Indian scalp. It was considered proof of death. If a man were scalped alive, however, he would not necessarily die, because if scalped by an Indian, all he would be missing was his scalplock—a two-inch circular patch from the crown of his head. Nevertheless, in the extravagance of battle many a man parted with more.

Just as each tribe had its own hair styles and customs, each had its own implements for arranging the hair. The Dakota used the flat five-inch tail of the Canada porcupine, while the Zuni of the Southwest used the fibers of the yucca. Eskimos fashioned combs from ivory, and the Iroquois made theirs from deer antlers.

Indians of all tribes loved to bedeck themselves with ornaments to add luster to their appearance. Some inserted objects directly into the lips, nose, or ears, while others hung jewelry around their necks, arms, legs, and waist.

Round ivory lip plugs, known as labrets, were worn with great pride by Eskimo men. At puberty a perforation was made at the corner of a boy's mouth and a round, button-like stud was inserted. As he got older, larger and larger labrets were inserted until the hole could accommodate one an inch in diameter. In winter, the men removed their lip plugs when they hunted, so the flesh would not freeze. But, following the dictates of vanity, they reinserted them upon entering a village.

Earrings were another delight. Not just one but sometimes ten or twelve were worn, so that the entire ear was covered. Large holes perforated the outer edge of the ear, from which baubles of copper, dried nuts, deer dew claws, or dentalium shells were hung. Later, glass beads and metals obtained through trade became popular.

Just about anything that was small and could be bored and strung was hung about the neck. Necklaces were fashioned from nuts, dried berries, animal bones, bird claws and beaks, the baby teeth of elk, antlers, horns, hooves, ivory, turquoise, pearls, clams, and conch shells.

Bear claws were the most coveted of all. They were rarely traded. A man had to get his own bear. And that was a feat second only to the taking of a scalp. The claws of the grizzly were the most valued, for he was the largest of the bears and, when attacked, a formidable opponent. The black bear was also taken for his claws, but was a lesser prize because of his relatively small size.

Wampum were beautifully carved beads, highly valued by the Indians. Colonial entrepreneurs, however, began to manufacture excessive quantities for trading in skins. As the market became flooded, the beads lost some of their value.

Until the British devalued wampum through mass production, its worth was determined by its color and finish. The crafting of a single shell required the highest degree of skill and it could be properly wrought only by the most practiced hand. Because it was found in such abundance, the purple and white shell of the clam *Venus mercenaria* was most frequently used. Wampum was ground from both the white and the purple, but the latter was twice as valuable.

Boring and shaping were meticulous processes, requiring great agility with the hand-bow and grinding stone. Drilling the hole was no small chore. It was done, however, before the shell was ground down to final size. To prevent heat caused by the friction of the drill from cracking the bead, drops of water were sprinkled on it throughout the process. The beads were bored through from each end, smoothed and shaped on a grindstone, and finally strung on sinew or grass.

Old wampum belts are cherished even today by the Iroquois and guarded with great care. Sacred belts commemorate the Old Way of Handsome Lake, a one-hundred-fifty-year-old religion still practiced today on Seneca and other reservations. The relics symbolize the days of the dim past, before the coming of colonists, when the League of the Iroquois was in its full splendor.

The photographs in this section show how the Indians looked and in what fashion they dressed themselves with clothes, paint, tattoos, feathers, and jewelry. The blending of European and Indian clothing styles, apparent in almost all the portraits, reflects, though on a very small scale, the powerful impact foreigners had on the first Americans.

By the time the camera was invented and pioneer photographers went west, many tribes had adopted articles of European clothing. Ready-made fabrics, buttons, and factory-produced trousers facilitated lives. Although the Indians did not realize it at the time, these things opened the way for further European influences that ultimately impoverished the Indian way of life.

Photography had its drawbacks. The wet-plate process could have helped to dispel some of the prevalent images about the Indians and correct the notion that the frontier was the "meeting point between savagery and civilization," as Frederick Jackson Turner later put it. Instead, the camera often furthered misapprehensions. Photographers frequently regarded — and therefore rendered — the Indians as gaudy showpieces and objects of civilized curios-ity. Although the portraits were subject to the predilections of the photographers, they can create new impressions for twentieth-century viewers. When we look at the images we can see one step farther back than the camera did and, with information made available by early explorers, missionaries, and ethnologists, glimpse a little more of the fullness of Indian life.

Tattoos, bear-claw necklaces, buffalo robes, goat-hair blankets all harken back to the days when the Indian was his own person, when man was a species that meshed so well with the pattern of the universe that he could not help but regard the spectacle of life with awe.

NORTHERN PAIUTE and ARAPAHO

Publicity photo taken during the filming of the silent-era

epic, "The Covered Wagon," in 1923, shows Wyoming Arapahoes

recruited for the movie (plus a white actor at far left)

with Jack Wilson (seated). Also known as Wovoka,

Wilson was the Paiute prophet who originated the messianic

movement popularly known as the Ghost Dance religion.

DAKOTA (Teton)
Grey Whirlwind conversing in sign language
with Ernest Thompson Seton, author and
illustrator of many books on wildlife
and woodcraft, in 1927.
They are seated outside a tepee at
the Standing Rock Reservation.
in North Dakota. Sign language
was used extensively among the Plains
tribes, whose spoken languages were mutually
incomprehensible. The sign for horse,
one of the most frequently used words,
was the index and middle fingers of the
right hand over the fingers of the left
symbolizing something ridden.
Clyde Fisher.

CROW

L to r: Poor Elk with a pipe; Black Foot wearing metal bracelets and holding a tomahawk; Long Ears with eagle-bone whistle, such as might be used in Sun Dance, and what appears to be either a pair of tweezers (for removing facial hair) or a metal whistle; He Shows His Face wearing a peace medal, possibly the Andrew Johnson issue of 1865; and Old Onion with pair of tweezers hanging from his necklace. Several have the light-colored blanket preferred in winter because it provided camouflage.

William Henry Jackson/Old Crow Agency on Yellowstone River, Montana/1871.

TONKAWA

Sherman Niles, with fur-wrapped braids and scalp lock, photographed at the Trans-Mississippi International Exposition at Omaha, Nebraska, in 1898. Niles' hair is his own, but some Indians often used false braids of horse hair for special occasions.

F. A. Rinehart/Bureau of American Ethnology.

UTE (Uintah Band)
Uintah Valley couple—"The
Warrior and His Bride" according
to the photographer—pose solemnly
on their home grounds, the
eastern slope of Utah's Wasatch
Range in the 1870s. The man wears a
hair-pipe breastplate, cartridge
belt, breechclout, and anklet.
His forelock is brushed up
and back in Plains fashion, and
it and his body are painted.
The young woman wears a beautifully
decorated over-the-shoulder
article whose use is unknown.

John K. Hillers/Powell Expedition/1872-74.

DAKOTA

Mrs. Left Hand and a small girl both wear cloth dresses, decorated with dentalium shells, and long belts with silver disks known as conchos. They were manufactured by whites for trade with Indians and were popular among many tribes during the later part of the nineteenth century. Mrs. Left Hand also has a hair-pipe necklace, a trade article made by whites from small bones.

Charles Henry Carpenter/Louisiana Purchase Exposition/St. Louis, Missouri/1904.

DAKOTA (Hunkpapa)

Sitting Bull poses, fierce and indomitable, at the height of his fame in 1885. It is nine years after Little Bighorn. He is 51. This year he endures the hoop-la of Buffalo Bill's Wild West Show, then returns to his people to lead the struggle to hold Dakota land. During the attempt to arrest him in December, 1890, on the Standing Rock Reservation, he was shot and killed. His death triggered the massacre at Wounded Knee.

David F. Barry/Bismarck, Dakota Territory/1885.

MANDAN

Eagle Woman works porcupine-quill designs into a hide, probably after 1900, when the art had become a rarity among the tribes. The quills were flattened, frequently between the teeth, and inserted into the hide. Glass beads, which traders exchanged with Indians for beaver pelts, eliminated most quillwork by the 1830s.

Photographer unknown.

KIOWA

Small girl's cloth dress is decorated with cowrie shells. The teeth of elk were frequently used as well. The cradleboard, holding her porcelain-faced doll, may be a replica of the one she was carried in as a baby.

Irwin and Mankins/Oklahoma Territory/1890s.

"SHETA-MO-ON-E"
A NOTED CHIEF OF YAKIMAS
COPYRIGHTED BY HUTTER
1900
THE TEPEE IS BUFALO SKINS

YAKIMA

Shetamoone, a chieftain, stands before a buffalo-skin tepee in full regalia. His buffalo-horned bonnet is decorated with weasel fur, and his braids are fur-wrapped. The bandolier across his chest has buttons, elk teeth, and mother-of-pearl disks. Both his costume and the tepee show the influence of the Plains culture on the southern region of the Columbia plateau.

Rutter/1900.

NEZ PERCE

Sophie Davis Broncheau with her daughter Louise in a cradleboard, probably at Lapwai, Idaho, between 1888 and 1892. Photographer Jane Gay was a talented amateur accompanying anthropologist Alice Fletcher. Fletcher was appointed by President Cleveland to oversee the division of land among the Nez Perce after the Dawes Act of 1887.

E. Jane Gay.

YUMA

Studio portrait of an Arizona-territory
Indian boy, his body painted with
white clay. The Yuma frequently
painted their bodies in
preparation for battle.

E. A. Bonine/Pasadena, California/1870s.

36

NEZ PERCE

Joseph Ratunda in Plains-style costume. Flaring roach atop his head is made of porcupine hair, and his otter-skin breastplate is decorated with trade mirrors. The white pelt probably is ermine. He has bells around his ankles.

Joseph Dixon/Wanamaker Expedition/1914.

NISENAN

Youth from Auburn, California, wears a bandeau of yellow-hammer feathers, an abalone gorget, and a sash decorated with bits of abalone. All of these were symbols of wealth.

Photographer unknown/1871-76.

PIMA

Lieta was photographed on the Gila River
Reservation in Arizona around 1901-02.
Her elaborate face paint is typical
of the women of many southwestern tribes
and may denote her family
or simply be adornmental.

Frank Russell/Sacaton, Arizona.

APACHE

This woman, Naltsoge-eh, has a mutilated nose. An
unfaithful wife might have her nose cut as punishment as well
as to make her less attractive. A widow who showed disrespect
to her husband's family by not observing a proper period of
mourning might have the end of her nose slashed. These
drastic measures were rarely used, however.

Probably A. Frank Randall or George Ben Wittick/1882-86.

SERI

Candelaria, an unmarried girl, wears face
paint denoting her family. Among the
Seri, this practice was almost entirely
confined to women, and the designs were
passed down from mother to daughter.

William Dinwiddie/Bureau of American Ethnology/
Rancho San Francisco de Costa Rica,
Sonora, Mexico/1894.

APACHE (Western, possibly Tonto)

Woman carries her baby on a cradleboard which
is supported by a tumpline across her chest. Babies were
placed on boards at about three months, completely laced
in when asleep (as here), but with arms free
when awake. Note the sun shade overhead. The mother's hair
is unusually short, a cut often used to mark the death of a relative.

W. J. Lubken/Bureau of Reclamation, Salt River Project, near Roosevelt, Arizona/1907.

APACHE

Rolling small hoops with long poles was a gambling game with ceremonial overtones played exclusively by men. Women were not allowed to play but, like the one in the background, they could watch.

Photographer unknown/San Carlos, Arizona/1899.

COCOPA

Young man of the tribe with ethnologist of the Bureau of American Ethnology. They are standing in front of what appears to be a willow branch house for summer. In winter the Cocopa lived in mud-plaster huts.

DeLancey Gill/Bureau of American Ethnology/ Sonora, Mexico/1900.

MARICOPA and MOHAVE

Seated Maricopas flank a
standing Mohave. The face paint
of the Mohave appears to
have been applied to
the negative after picture
was taken, a technique
used by some photographers
to make their subjects
appear more exotic.

E. A. Bonine/Pasadena, California/1876.

NAVAJO

Old warrior poses with a lance
and a painted shield. Braves of some
tribes painted shields
with their most sacred
designs to imbue
them with power to ward
off bullets and arrows.

James Mooney/Bureau
of American Ethnology/near Keam's Canyon,
Navajo Reservation, Arizona/1893.

Governor of San F...

SAN FELIPE

Many tribes of the Southwest used pump drills, such as the one here, to bore holes in beads. Contrary to the simpler bow drill, the twirling action was constant. When the cross bar was pressed down it caused the buckskin thongs to twist the drill, and upon release caused it to rotate in the other direction.

John K. Hillers/Bureau of American Ethnology/San Felipe Pueblo, New Mexico/about 1880.

NAVAJO

An old woman is spinning wool, probably for a blanket like that on the woman at right. Until the Spanish introduced sheep, blankets were made of cotton. Note the hand-rotated spindle.

James Mooney/Bureau of American Ethnology/near Keam's Canyon, Navajo Reservation, Arizona/1893.

HOPI

Unlike other groups, the Pueblo Indians of the Southwest assigned the task of weaving to men. The loom is vertical, unlike the Spanish horizontal type, and of ancient origin.

John K. Hillers/Bureau of American Ethnology/probably 1879.

NAVAJO

Americanization of an Indian: Tom Torleno
as he entered Carlisle School in Pennsylvania (left) and
as he appeared three years later. Carlisle
was founded by the Government in 1879 to teach
Indians the ways of white men. Those who learned
their lessons often found they no longer fitted
into their tribal structure. During summer,
when school was out, Indians often were not
permitted to go home, but were boarded in white
homes as domestic servants.

YAVAPAI

Studio portrait shows the tremendous changes
in the appearance of southwestern Indians by the
1880s. The man on the left wears a buckskin shirt
decorated with narrow lines of beadwork and silver
conchos in the Southern Plains manner. Moccasin
boots with turned-up toes were typical of Apaches,
and trousers of man on right are like the
pair-a-year allotted by the Government to some reservation
Indians. By the nineties, practically every
western male, Indian or white, wore a cartridge belt.

A. Miller/1880s or 90s.

NOOTKA

Chief Moqwinna, in uniform, with a double-barreled shotgun, is flanked by two men and a woman at Friendly Cove, Nootka Sound, Vancouver Island, British Columbia.

Photographer unknown/1896.

COLVILLE

Hudson's Bay blanket, which this woman wears, was a popular trade item. The Colville, a tribe on the Columbia plateau, were named for a fort built in 1826 for Eden Colvile, a director of Hudson's Bay Company.

Photographer unknown/before 1900.

TLINGIT (Sitka)

Alaskan Indian, Sitka Jake, wears Chilkat blanket of mountain-goat hair and cedar fibers. The ceremonial headdress is a carved wooden plaque painted and inlaid with shell and feathers. Sea-lion whiskers protrude from top; sides and back are covered with ermine. Wooden rattle filled with pebbles has carved raven with reclining man on its back.

Photographer unknown/about 1900.

ESKIMO

Men from Icy Cape, Alaska, wear their highly valued ornamental lip plugs—
or labrets—made of ivory, bone, jade, or other stones. The lip was pierced
during adolescence, and the hole enlarged by progressively larger plugs.

E. W. Nelson/1877-81.

ESKIMO (Togiagamiut)

An old woman from Togiak, Alaska, wears a jacket made from skins of the double-crested cormorant. It is warm and light, but fragile. A young woman would make hers with a pouch on the back in which to carry her baby.

Henry B. Collins/U.S. National Museum/1927.

UPPER ATNA or UPPER TANANA

Group of women and children.
"Butch" is smoking a curio or trade
pipe whose bowl is a carved Indian
head. The hat of the boy in foreground,
as well as the dress of little girl
at left, have bone-button decorations,
probably obtained from
traders along the Yukon River.

Miles Brothers/1902.

SEMINOLE

Woman with child wears long skirt
and large collar made from cotton strips
joined by a sewing machine. Her many
strands of beads were a vogue of
the time. This costume came into fashion
in the late 19th century.

Byrons/Florida/before late 1916.

POWHATAN (Chickahominy)

Turn-of-century family in Virginia
poses for portrait in non-Indian dress.

James Mooney/Bureau of American Ethnology/
Chickahominy River/1900.

SEMINOLE

Daguerreotype, probably taken in New Orleans in 1852, is a portrait of Billy Bowlegs, a leader of Seminoles in the Third Seminole War (1856-58). His costume is derived from 18th-century styles. Born in 1812, Bowlegs was captured at the end of the war and deported via New Orleans to Indian Territory, where he died in 1863-64. The Seminoles were originally Lower Creeks, allies of the Spanish who fled to Florida during the 18th century to escape British attacks. Their name was derived from the Creek word meaning fugitive.

Photographer unknown/1852. Courtesy of Theodore Les'ey.

Dance before a stick-ball game in 1888.
Women dancers stand behind the leader seated with a
drum, and the male players stand around a fire. The dance
leader of the men is at the left shaking a gourd rattle.
Ball sticks, similar to those used in lacrosse, hang on rack.

James Mooney/Bureau of American Ethnology/Qualla Reservation, North Carolina.

POWHATAN (Pamunkey)
Bradbys, Cooks, Dennis's,
and Allmonds—Indians
whose ancestors
intermarried with whites.
William Bradby, with bow and
tomahawk, could
trace his family back to 1720.

DeLancey Gill/Bureau of American
Ethnology/Pamunkey Reservation,
Virginia/October 1899.

SAUK

Earliest photograph in the book,
a daguerreotype of Keokuk, a
war chief against the British
during the War of 1812. He wears a
turban, hair roach, ball-and-cone
ear ornaments, and bear-claw
and dentalium shell necklaces.
By the time this was taken,
the Sauk had been evacuated
from the Old Northwest to
Indian Territory. Keokuk died the
year following this picture.

Thomas M. Easterly/Liberty, Missouri/1847.

ABENAKI (Passamaquoddy)

Three Maine Indians with a priest.
The man on the right wears a silver
headband. Belts and sashes are
plain and bead-embroidered.

Photographer unknown/1860-75. **61**

WAY THEY LIVED

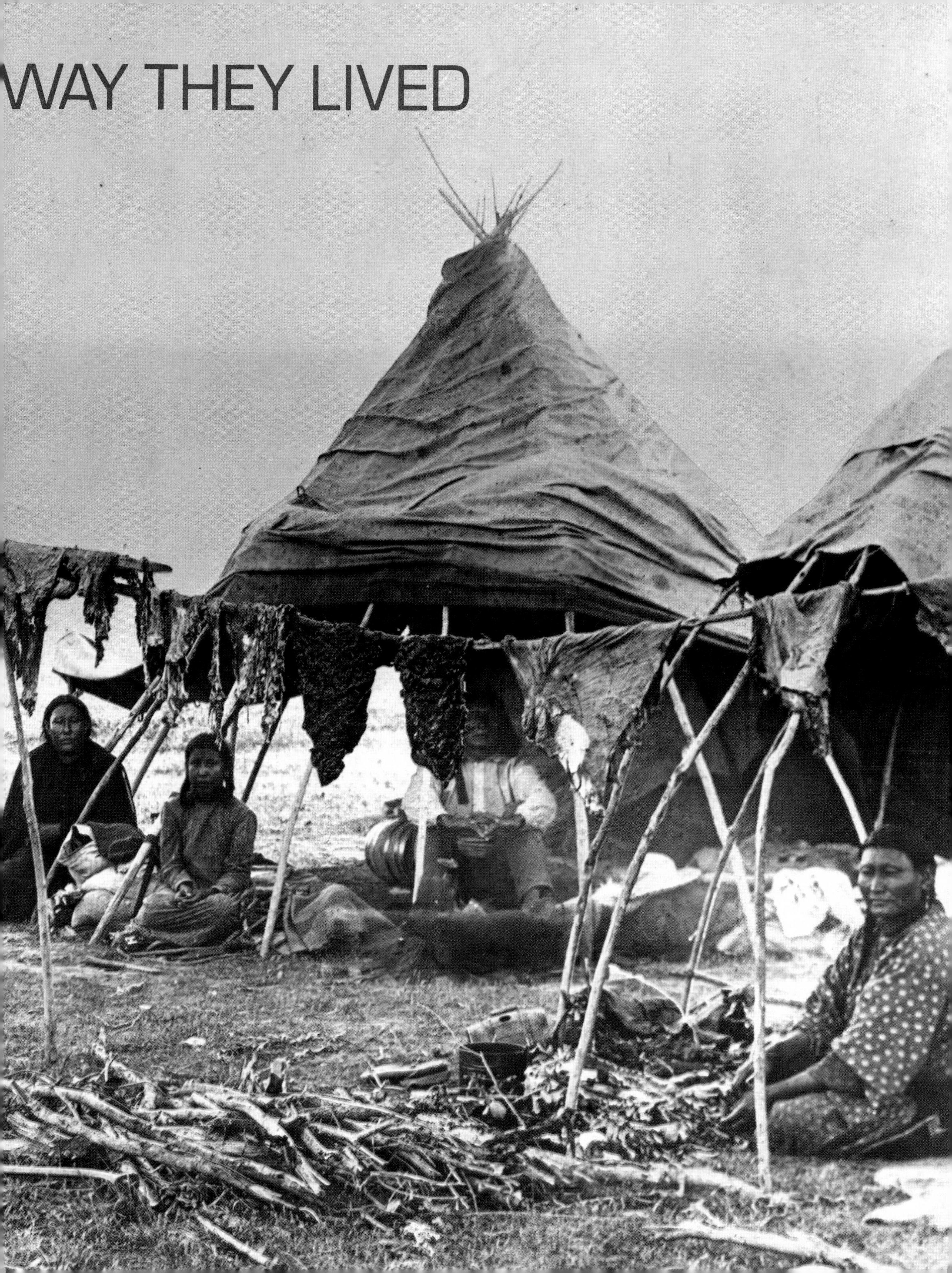

Each tribe, in its own way, revered the bounty of nature. To many Indians the earth was their mother, the mountains her bones, and the grass her hair. They never defiled the land or altered the balance of wildlife to their own ends, but lived instead in a perpetual bond of kinship, a relationship which they respected profoundly and reenacted in ceremonies of great moment.

Throughout their culture the people devised ingenious ways to exist in their particular environment. Whether woodland or tundra, grassland or desert, the natural life of each area molded the existence of the people. They ate the plants and animals the land supported and slept in shelters made from the raw materials it furnished.

Above all, food was the essential. Its abundance or scarcity determined how long a tribe stayed in one place and in what kind of dwelling. The Dakota of the Great Plains, for example, lived in portable tepees because they followed the buffalo migrations in a constant hunt for flesh and hides. The Navajo of the Southwest, however, stayed year after year in permanent houses of sticks covered with sod to tend crops and herd sheep.

Although the richness of Indian life can never be completely captured, information about food, housing, customs, and religious ceremonies is available. One of the best sources is the pictures of early photographers who followed the frontier and set up shop in railheads or mining towns along the way.

William Henry Jackson was typical in many ways of the young men who entered the Indian territories, but his ability to capture in the microcosm of his camera both the westward movement of the Nation and the changing ways of the Indians was unique. Jackson headed out from Keeseville, New York, in 1866, and when he reached St. Louis hired out as a bullwhacker driving prairie schooners along the Overland Trail. He decided to settle in Omaha, where construction on the Union Pacific was beginning, and with his forty-pound camera followed its westward path. He missed the moment, however, when the golden spike joined East to West at Promontory Point, Utah, because May 10, 1869, was his wedding day and, as he says in his autobiography, *Time Exposure*, since his bride was doing him the favor he did not think he should miss the event.

He was not the only young man with a camera to seek fame and fortune in the West. Some went with government surveys, others sought gold and silver, and still others went as missionaries or teachers to reservations. Somewhere along the line almost all the wet-plate practitioners photographed the Indians of the Great Plains.

After the Indians were forced off their lands, the Bureau of Reclamation became interested in what was known at the time as the Great American Desert for irrigation projects, and H. T. Cory, a photographer for the Bureau, took many pictures of how the Plains tribes lived once they were on reserves.

Before they were exterminated, buffalo were the substance of life for many of the Plains people. Until horses revolutionized the chase in the 1700s, the Indians hunted on foot. Camouflaged in bison robes or wolf skins, they crawled downwind until within shooting range. An arrow had to hit dead on, because the hunters, encumbered by their disguises, could not discharge their bows quickly. The Buffalo Indians also stampeded small herds over precipices by frightening them with fires.

Horses changed all that. Herds became far more accessible and the take was easily transported back to camp. Techniques of

Preceding pages: CHEYENNE
Meat drying on racks at a
Cheyenne summer
camp in 1895 probably is beef.
By that time few buffalo were
in Cheyenne country,
and the U.S. Government
supplied Indians with beef.
Many tribes
continued to prepare it as they
had buffalo. Intestines, which were
cleaned and stuffed
as sausages, hang at
the left, and a woman works
unprepared entrails at the right
Photographer and location unknown/1895.

the kill changed with rapid fire. Arrows were shot in uninterrupted volleys at full gallop, and agile ponies became essential to the buffalo culture.

Bison meat was the Plains Indians' favorite food. Thin strips of meat were hung in the sun to dry on racks high off the ground, so dogs could not reach them, for they too found buffalo tasty. Sometimes the dried strips were eaten plain, in which case it was called jerky, or it was pounded and mixed with hot grease and dried berries for extra flavor. This was pemmican. It would keep for years without spoiling in bags of buffalo-bladders and was an ideal food for the nomadic tribes. They also roasted fresh flesh over coals of buffalo chips and broiled intestine sausages.

Buffalo not only furnished the Indians with food, but supplied the fuel with which to cook it. Wood was scarce and dried dung was everywhere; observers reported that it made a sweet-smelling fire.

Equally important were the hides, which were made into clothes and shelter. The dressing of the skin was an art, usually performed by the women of the tribe, and was such a vital skill that a woman's tanning ability was frequently taken into equal account with her beauty when she was chosen as a bride.

There were numerous steps to the preparation of a hide and each required a different tool. First the skin was staked out either on the ground or on a vertical frame. Next came the fleshing process. Meat left on the hide by the skinner was carefully scraped off with a buffalo leg-bone. Then, if the skin was to be used for a tepee, the hair was removed with an adze and saved for cushion stuffing. If it was to be a robe, the hair remained. Then brains and liver were mixed with melted fat and worked through the skin, which was sub-

sequently soaked in water. The next day the excess liquid was stripped out with a long stone blade and the hide hung out to dry. Sometimes it was smoked over a fire to make it more waterproof. Once all the moisture had evaporated, the brittle leather was scraped with the spongy joint of a thigh bone and rubbed back and forth across a sinew rope to make it supple.

A tepee required eight to twenty skins sewn together with sinew in a semicircular shape. They were then laid around wooden poles stuck into the ground to form a cone. One was never in danger of being smoked out in a tepee because the direction of the top opening could be shifted by means of long sticks with the slightest change of the wind.

Not all the Plains Indians hunted constantly for buffalo. Some sought them only in summer and winter, and tended crops the other two seasons. Because they always returned to their planted corn fields, they built permanent houses, but when they went abroad on the great chase they set up camps of portable skin-tepees. The Caddo and Wichita of the southern Plains, where grass was plentiful, covered theirs with thatch, and the Omaha and Pawnee of the central Plains, where shorter grass with longer roots was abundant, made sod-covered earth lodges.

Wily white men knew that the end of the buffalo meant the end of Plains culture. When General Phil Sheridan was asked to support a Congressional movement in the 1870s to prevent the extinction of the herds by white hunters who sold hides at $3 apiece for fur coats and carriage robes back east, he said, "The best way to get rid of the Indian is to destroy the buffalo by which he lives. The more buffaloes killed, the better, and what good is a buffalo anyway except for slaughter."

When the buffalo were gone the Plains Indians had to give up their tepees of hide, their clothes of softly tanned leather, and their delicious pemmican. They lived instead on reservations in tepees of canvas, wore mass-produced pants and shirts of factory-made cotton, and ate Texas beef, all supplied by the United States Government. Even the canvas tepees did not last long. The government insisted on replacing them with flimsy wooden shacks in an attempt to "civilize" the Indians. The chief who cooperated with the government had a relatively lavish house. A comfortable chief, it was reasoned, was likely to keep discontented tribesmen in line.

As part of the national reconnaissance to aid western settlers, Government explorers photographed and studied extensively the conditions of the arid Southwest. One thing that especially interested them was how the Indians managed to live off land that had little water and supported few game animals. Some of the photographs we have today are from their research, and also from the findings of the Bureau of Reclamation, which surveyed the area beginning in 1899 to determine the potential for irrigation.

Water was the paramount problem for the people of the Southwest. The rain clouds traveling east from the Pacific Coast unleash their burden on the Sierra Nevadas and, as a result, the Colorado plateau receives an average of only ten inches of rainfall a year.

The Hopi stored water in large round earthen jars fashioned by hand from the rich clay earth without the rounding motion of a potter's wheel. The main drawback to the clay ware was that it broke easily, and although a jar could be replaced, its water could not. Consequently, water was gathered from streams in containers made of tightly woven willow splints covered with pine resin so they would not leak. The Zuni, however, irrigated their crops by carrying water to the plots in beautifully decorated pottery vessels and sprinkling the delicate shoots by hand.

Both the Hopi and the Zuni lived well off their land. They planted small vine and root crops, such as squash, pumpkins, peppers, onions, garlic, and beans, that did not require much water. Archaeologists estimate that they had been doing so for at least two thousand years. For millennia corn has been their most important food, and a primitive variety known as maize (Zea mays) was cultivated as long as five thousand years ago. It was ground and eaten as gruel, hominy, mush, and bread. Even yeast was derived from chewed corn, which reacted chemically with saliva.

Cooking reached a rather high art among the Hopi and Zuni, and before the Spaniards introduced dome-shaped ovens with draft holes on top, many of the Pueblo tribes baked their food in large pits. Stones or gravel in the bottom were heated by fire and, after the fire had burned itself out, food was placed on top and covered with leaves and dirt.

Hunting in the Southwest was minimal because of the scarcity of large animals. The eating of fish was strictly forbidden by many tribes, and bear and beaver were prohibited by the Apache and Navajo. Jackrabbits, however, were frequently hunted with a special curved stick, hurled through the air with unerring accuracy.

Sedentary pueblo-dwelling tribes of the Southwest lived in large, flat-roofed adobe houses, built several stories high, which were entered by means of an outside ladder. Houses in the western part of the region, near the Little Colorado River, were made of stone covered with mud, and those to the east, near the Rio Grande, where stone was scarce, were made of large sun-dried bricks.

Not all tribes southwest of the Rocky Mountains lived in pueblos, however. Some regions, such as the Great Basin, lacked clay or stone, or both. The Western Shoshone and Paiute of the Basin slept in hastily-built brush huts intended only to protect them from the wolves and winds of the night. During the day, they scavenged for crickets, snakes, and roots for food, and stayed in one locality only as long as food was available.

The United States acquired many of the small islands off the west coast of Canada from Britain in 1846 and from Russia twenty-one years later with the purchase of Alaska. The Federal Government was never particularly interested in the area because it was inaccessible and the islands too small to accommodate masses of westbound settlers. The first survey group, dispatched in 1841, took three years to get there, because the ship had to go around Cape Horn.

The discovery of gold on the Frazer River in 1859 did bring prospectors into the region in hopes of a bonanza like that of forty-nine, and among them Richard Maynard, who became one of the principal photographers of Northwest Coast Indians. Maynard had been a shoemaker in Ontario before the gold rush and, when findings proved to be only a flash in the pan, he returned home to find that in his absence his wife had opened a photography studio. He too learned the trade, and together they went to the Northwest, this time in search of the natural abundance of wilderness life.

The problems of existence along the coast did not arise from scarcity. Quite the opposite. Rain was plentiful, fish teemed in the rivers, sea otters and whales abounded in the ocean, cedars and spruce grew to magnificent heights, and the woods were filled with elk, deer, and warblers.

Cutting a two-hundred-foot red cedar was a mean task and, before European trappers and traders arrived, the Indians had no iron for axes or saws. Lacking both, they felled the mighty trees—often twenty feet across—with heavy wooden hammers and antler wedges. The tree was then rolled down to the water and floated to the village, where it was cut up. The cedar provided not only wood for houses, boats, and fires, but also bark for clothing, fishing lines, nets, and baskets.

The long houses could accommodate up to fifty people. Usually one family of three or four generations lived in each house, which was broken up inside into many rooms. Houses built before the nineteenth century had rough vertical planks secured with pegs of wood or antler, whereas those built later had planed horizontal boards joined with nails.

Fish were the mainstay of the Northwest Coast Indians' diet, and without cedar for boats, spears, hooks, and lines they would have been nearly impossible to catch. Giant canoes, holding up to twenty-five people, were made by gouging out a tree with fire, water, and stone adzes. Huge fishing parties went out in them in search of all the sea had to offer.

Pacific salmon abounded. Weighing up to a hundred pounds, *Oncorhynchus tshawytscha* was such an important part of the Chinook tribe's diet that it is known today as the Chinook salmon. In fact, the tribe gave its name to several savory dishes, including Chinook olives, which are acorns ripened in a pit of urine.

Inland tribes speared salmon in rivers on their annual spawning run. Strategically placed wooden dams blocked their passage upstream, and sometimes steeped hemlock bark was added to the water to stupefy them and slow their movement. Then they were speared. Eggs were taken from the belly of females and preserved in the ground for months at a time before eating.

Eels were another favorite. They were best caught by night when feeding on nightcrawlers, minnows, or worms. Bark traps were used, or lines of twinned pine-root with a sharp wooden splinter on the end concealed in minnow bait.

Throughout the country, the Government sponsored expeditions to find what the earth and its waters would yield for the needs of the burgeoning Nation. One of the main sources of information about the Eskimos and Indians along the Alaskan and Canadian coasts came in the 1890s from observations by the Bureau of Fisheries, which was interested in the possibilities for whaling. The Bureau studied the whaling techniques of the Eskimos and at the same time took pictures of how they lived.

Whales were to the Eskimo what buffalo were to the Plains Indians. The giant sea-mammals furnished them with food, fuel, clothing, and baleen beams for their dome-shaped earth-houses. The odds against survival in the Arctic were tremendous and, through supreme inventiveness, the people put each part of the whale to use.

The bowhead whale (*Baleana mysticetus*), which reaches fifty feet and fifty tons when full grown, was sought with great vigor and commonly known as The Whale.

A two-year-old, from eight to twenty feet in length, was preferred for eating because it had more juicy fat than an adult. In fact, the name for a two-year-old is "ingutuk," which means "best food."

The carcass was put to many uses. Most important, fat was used for fuel. The ribs and baleen served as structural supports, and membranes surrounding large organs were used as containers in which to boil water. Because a membrane bag could not be heated directly above a fire, hot stones were submerged, instead, to make the liquid boil.

The source of food determined where the Eskimo lived, and the resources available dictated what his dwellings were made of. Houses varied from region to region but, for the most part, they were of three main types: tents of caribou skin for summer, when the Eskimos were off hunting in the interior; igloos used in winter while traveling; and permanent earth-lodges for winter, when they fished. Some tribes, such as the Caribou Eskimo at the western edge of Hudson Bay, lived in igloos in winter and caribou tents in summer and hunted caribou all year.

Government employees were by no means the only people with cameras in the Arctic and Subarctic at the turn of the century. Many photographs were taken by pioneers who became commercial photographers. A certain F. H. Nowell was in Nome, Alaska, in 1905, and one can only guess precisely what took him and his camera there. Gold dust was found that year along the beaches of Nome, and in a year the population reached 12,000. Only two years before it had been an unknown settlement, whose designation on maps as "Name?" came to be misread as Nome. Thousands of prospectors swarmed in, and many hit pay dirt, earning as much as $1,000 a day. The boom brought in saloons, gambling houses, fancy women, vigilantes, and even Wyatt Earp.

Whatever it was that took Nowell to Nome, he serves as an example of the unknown pioneer photographer following the frontier, recording it, and being an integral part of it.

It was only natural, as people became interested in the clothing, food, crafts, and houses of the various tribes, that the scholars would become fascinated by their languages, customs, and ceremonies, which often expressed implicitly the meaning of a tribe's existence.

A few photographers, such as Matilda Coxe Stevenson, the anthropologist who burst into a sacred Zuni kiva, or ceremonial hut, during a secret Galaxy Fraternity ceremony, captured very authentic pictures. Others took shots that were posed. Such was Edward Curtis, commissioned by J. P. Morgan at the turn of the century to photograph all the tribes of North America. Curtis emphasized the all-encompassing ceremonial aspect of Indian life but, because by that time many of the old traditions had died out or been suppressed, his subjects were often posed.

The Sun Dance was of special interest to photographers and scholars of Indian lore both because it was practiced in many different forms throughout the Great Plains, and because it was a splendid spectacle. The name came not from worship of the sun, but from the Dakota word for the celebration, meaning "sun-gazing." People stared at the sun before beginning their hours of frenzied dancing. Among some tribes the Sun Dance was held once a year, in late summer, for what was usually four days of fasting and four days of dancing, frequently as a fulfillment of a vow made to the spirits. It was also, through the intervention of spirits, intended to insure the perpetuation of the great bison and the well-being of the tribe.

Self-torture was one of the principal ordeals a brave underwent to beseech his own spirit to guard him in war and aid him in the hunt, and fasting was the most important. Two tortures were especially prevalent, each preceded by long periods of abstinence from food. The first was the insertion of a wooden skewer, attached by a long rope to a high pole, through a man's chest. He then leaned backward and, after a period of straining, ripped his flesh from the skewer. Among the Mandan, a brave would dangle from a high pole until the weight of his body pulled out the skewer. The other method, equally painful, was similar. A skewer attached by rope to a buffalo head was run through the flesh of the shoulder. The warrior had to drag the head along the ground until the sharp instrument tore free.

The Sun Dance varied from tribe to tribe, but many had symbolic elements in common. Most tribes placed their tepees in a semicircle which opened toward the east, and each tepee had its own entrance pointed east, the direction from which divine help came.

Rain was the life-giving fluid to the tribes of the Southwest; it made the earth blossom and the crops flourish. Its scarcity made it a great blessing, and ceremonies were held to cleanse the world, so the blessed rain would be free to fall on pure land.

The Hopi enacted a Snake Dance every other year as a prayer for the precious liquid. Members of the secret Snake Society danced with rattlesnakes in their mouths. The people believed the snakes to be their relatives and intermediaries between them and the gods.

Preceremonial and initiation rites were held in kivas, which admitted only secret society members to the sacred chambers, for eight days prior to the dance. During a ceremony, dry paintings of mythical and sacred animals were made on the floor of a kiva with finely powdered sandstone and charcoal. The designs were elaborate and ritualistic in their execution, and believed to cure the sick and insure the welfare of the tribe.

The remote northwest coast of Canada was a haven for ethnologists, such as Franz Boas, at the end of the nineteenth century, because the passage of time and the advent of Europeans had had little effect on traditional Indian customs and ceremonies. Indians along the coast honored the spirits for the abundance of nature by giving away their own possessions with equal generosity. Potlatch, as it was called, was a part of the winter cycle of ceremonies. It paid homage to and insured the fecundity of the spirits of the region, and magnificent gifts of goat-hair blankets and copper plates were given away. A man might divest himself of everything but his house, although, in his mind, he would be richer for the prestige accrued from the generosity of his gifts. In subsequent ceremonies it was customary that he be repaid in kind and with interest, so that actually no one was impoverished.

Totem poles were sometimes erected during the potlatch ceremonies. They were a rather recent development in the culture of the coastal Indians, because wood-carving reached its peak, especially among the Haida, only after iron-edged tools were introduced by foreigners. A pole placed directly in front of a house was an outward sign of wealth, and had crests of bears, eagles, and beaver, often denoting family history, chiselled on them by highly paid artisans.

Among all the tribes, intricate ritual and mysterious taboos permeated all phases of life. The taking and eating of food, the curing of disease, the rites of birth, puberty, marriage, and death were all elaborately interlaced with the guardian spirits of the universe.

Some diseases were thought to be caused by spirits who had been insulted by the disregard of men. One had to be very careful; the smallest slight could bring disaster. A menstruating Haida woman could not cross a stream lest the Old Woman at the source remove the fish. A Creek could not show disrespect to a fire by spitting on it. A hunting Seneca had to propitiate the spirit of the beaver before he killed one. If disregarded, each of these spirits might punish the offender with illness and, if the offense were serious enough, pestilence might strike the tribe.

Among many southeastern tribes, the entry of an offended animal into a person's body caused a disease which, among the Creeks, was known by the animal's name. One of the problems besetting a medicine man was to locate the part of the body where the beast had lodged itself. Once discovered, the evil spirit was exorcised by special ceremonies.

Although shamanistic practices involved whistles, drums, rattles, and sacred medicine bundles containing such fetishes as deer tails or, among a few Cheyenne, dried human fingers to conjure out deleterious spirits, the medicine men's knowledge of pharmacology was amazingly thorough and their cures often effective. Angelica relieved stomach aches among the Creek; butterfly weed cured dysentery among the Catawba; and steeped bark of elm stopped coughs among the Mohegan.

Every aspect of a person's life, from birth to death, was a part of his surroundings, and the bond between man and his environment was constantly reinforced. Soon after a child was born he was given a name, a metaphor of what he was. As he grew older his name changed with him. Among many eastern and Plains tribes, a boy reaching the age of fifteen fasted for several days and then embarked on a quest for his guardian spirit. The spirit, appearing to him in a vision, gave him the name that was to be his, and he was to be, for the rest of his time. The spirit also imparted protective symbols to paint on his body and songs to sing before going into battle. Then he could take his place among the warriors.

Death spirits were a vital influence in Indian life. Southern Ute bands burned the dwellings and clothes of the dead, along with the corpse, so its ghost would rest in peace and not return to haunt the living. An old man of importance among the Salish of the Northwest Coast would be sequestered in a special hut to wait for death, and when it came he was placed on an elevated cedar canoe facing the ocean, west of which was the home of the spirits of the dead.

Many Indians of the Great Plains left their dead in trees, while some tribes of the Southeast embalmed corpses and kept them in burial huts.

A new religion born of deep despair, known as the Ghost Dance, arose in 1888 partially as a result of Government suppression of ages-old ceremonies and the resulting cultural disintegration. The Ghost Dance started among the Paiute and within a year spread throughout the West. It expressed, through incessant dancing and chanting, the belief that the white usurpers would disappear and the Indians would inherit the earth, and once again walk proudly on their land.

In the view of whites it was a subversive movement to be quashed, along with all other vestiges of Indian culture. The agent of Standing Rock Reservation ordered Sitting Bull arrested by Indian police for supposedly leading the movement among the Dakota. During the struggle that ensued, both Sitting Bull and his son were killed, and panic seized the other Indians. Big Foot and his tiny band of men, women, and children tried to flee, but were shot down by mounted troops in the massacre at Wounded Knee.

ASSINIBOIN

The painted medicine tepee of an Indian
named Nosey is made of canvas. The heavy
cotton was supplied to reservations by
the Government after the 1880s, when the
buffalo had been killed off and skins
could no longer be used. Canvas can be
easily recognized by the few
pieces joined together with even seams.

Sumner W. Matteson/Fort Belknap Reservation,
Montana/July 1906.

ARAPAHO

The irregular patches and heavy seams show that this tepee was made from
buffalo hides. The black at the top is not decoration but the inside
flap turned out. It has become blackened from the smoke of buffalo-chip fires.

William S. Soule/about 1867-74.

DAKOTA

Men are seated in a sweat lodge with its covering partly raised, showing the willow frame. Rocks in the foreground were heated, brought into the lodge, and sprinkled with water to produce steam. Before tin buckets, water was carried into the sweat lodge in a buffalo stomach. Sweating was both social activity and a pre-ceremonial purification.

Jesse Hastings Bratley/Lower Cut Meat Camp School, Rosebud Reservation, South Dakota/1898.

WICHITA

Three kinds of shelter: an open-sided thatched structure for cooking, a grass house for sleeping, and a frame for a tepee used on buffalo hunts. The plot in the foreground was probably for corn.

Photographer unknown/probably before 1900.

COMANCHE

Hoof in the foreground and the time (1895) suggest these women and children are eating beef. Special delicacies included raw liver, brains, kidney, tripe, and leg-bone marrow.

Irwin and Mankins/Chickasha, Oklahoma Territory/about 1895.

PAWNEE

A village of earth lodges made of sod. Photographer Jackson said they could accommodate some 2500 people. The crowd probably is watching a ceremony. The blur in the right background is an American flag.

William Henry Jackson/Loup Fork of the Platte, Nebraska/1868-69.

ARK HOUSE

SAUK and FOX

An elm-bark lodge was a permanent dwelling, large enough to accommodate several generations of one family. It was occupied each spring after fall and winter hunting and trapping. Originally, the Sauk and Fox were principally located around Green Bay, where they built lodges of elm near river-bottom fields. When the tribes were removed to the marshlands of the Indian Territory, after the Black Hawk War, they adapted their old ways to the new climate.

William S. Prettyman/Indian Territory/1880s. 79

COMANCHE (Kwahadi)
Quanah Parker and his wife
Tonicy on the verandah of
their home in Oklahoma
Territory in the 1890s. Son of
a Kwahadi chief and a
captive white woman,
Parker was born about 1845.
He became a war leader, and was
the last Comanche chief to
surrender. Becoming the head
man of the tribe on the reservation
in 1875, he visited Washington
often. He was one of three Indian
judges appointed to the Court of
Indian Offenses set up in the
Indian Territory in the 1880s. He
also helped spread the peyote
religion among Plains tribes at
the end of the 19th century.
He died in 1911.

Hutchins or Lanney/Bureau of American Ethnolo
Kiowa Reservation/Oklahoma Territory/1891-93.

CROW

A well-to-do Indian family at dinner.
Traditional dress and hair styles are in contrast
to the "white" dining-room setting. The picture probably was
taken on a reservation, where Indian leaders
often were given the best housing
to keep them comfortable and uncomplaining.

Richard Throssel/Bureau of Reclamation/1910.

DAKOTA

Indians assemble to get beef on ration
day at Fort Yates in the Standing Rock Reservation, Dakota
Territory. After the destruction of the buffalo culture and
establishment of cattle towns and railheads, herds were driven up from Texas.
Every two weeks cattle were corralled and shot by Indian
policemen. White clerks allotted the beef to the families.
Photographer unknown/late 1880s.

YAKIMA

Although they may have been the first,
the Plains Indians were not the only
people to build tepees. The Yakima of
the Columbia plateau adopted the shape
to the ecology of their area by using a
rush-mat covering instead of buffalo hide.

Possibly W. J. Lubken/Bureau of Reclamation/1907.

UMATILLA

Occasionally Indians of the Columbia plateau went into the Great Plains
to hunt buffalo, but their main food was fish. Salmon, rainbow trout,
and eel were preferred. Here fish hang out to dry.

Major Lee Moorhouse/Umatilla Reservation, Oregon/about 1900. **85**

PAIUTE

The Paiute were constantly on the move in summer in search of seasonal foods. A village encampment, such as this one Major Powell discovered on the Rio Virgin, a tributary of the Colorado, in southern Utah, provided temporary shelter for a few days before the band moved on.

John K. Hillers/Powell Expedition/near St. George, Utah/1872-74.

SERI

A family group beside a brush dwelling. From left: Juana Maria, matron of the house, a child without face paint, three girls (with paint), and the matron's brother (with hat). Designs on the cheeks are decorative.

William Dinwiddie/Bureau of American Ethnology/Rancho San Francisco de Costa Rica, Sonora, Mexico/1894.

SANTO DOMINGO

Panoramic view of the pueblo soon after the tracks of the Sante Fe Railroad, in the foreground, were laid. Not until the next year, 1880, did they reach Santa Fe. The tallest building is a church, probably built by Spanish missionaries. One of the photographer's cameras, on its tripod, is between the two wagons.

John K. Hillers/Bureau of American Ethnology/1879.

ZUNI

Five stories was about as high as the terraced architecture
of a pueblo ever went. There were no stairs inside, so
wooden ladders were propped against the outside walls.
Translucent mineral slabs were sometimes
used in windows for glass.

90 John K. Hillers/Bureau of American Ethnology/New Mexico/1879.

NAVAJO

Two women and girl are wearing what became traditional
dress after the introduction of sewing machines on the Navajo
reservation. They are standing in front of what is probably a
Government building on the reservation, because most Navajos lived
in sod-covered huts called hogans.

Bureau of Reclamation/Navajo Agency, Window Rock, Arizona/about 1900-20.

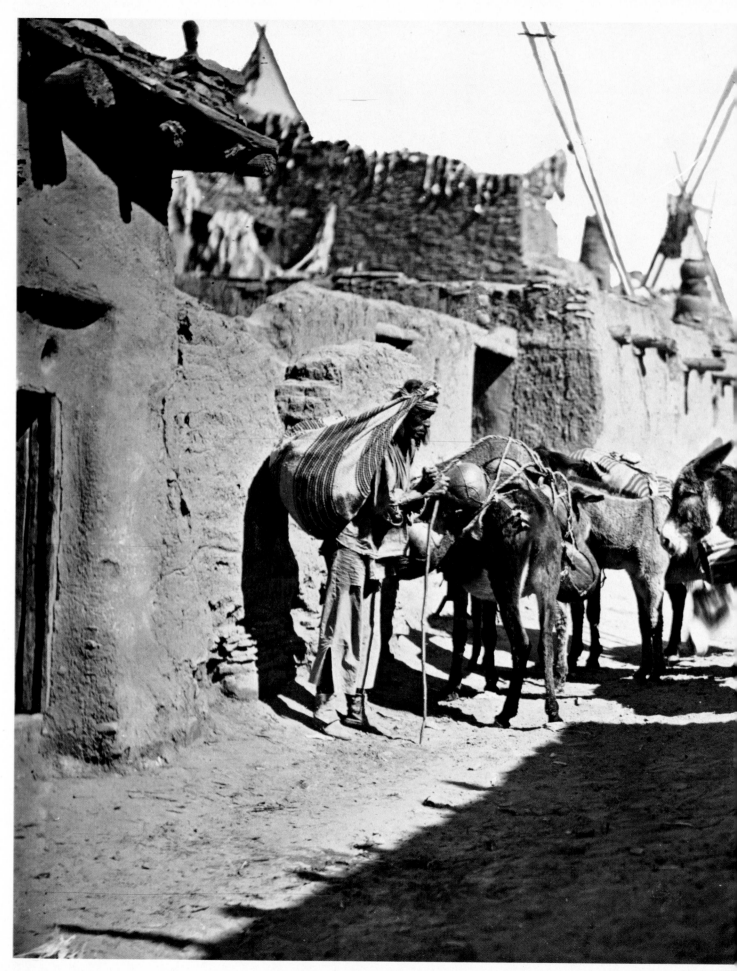

ZUNI

Burros being loaded in a
pueblo street. Most livestock
—horses, cattle, sheep, and
burros—were introduced to Indian
cultures by Spaniards in 1500s.

John K. Hillers/Bureau of American Ethnology/Zuni
Pueblo/New Mexico/1879.

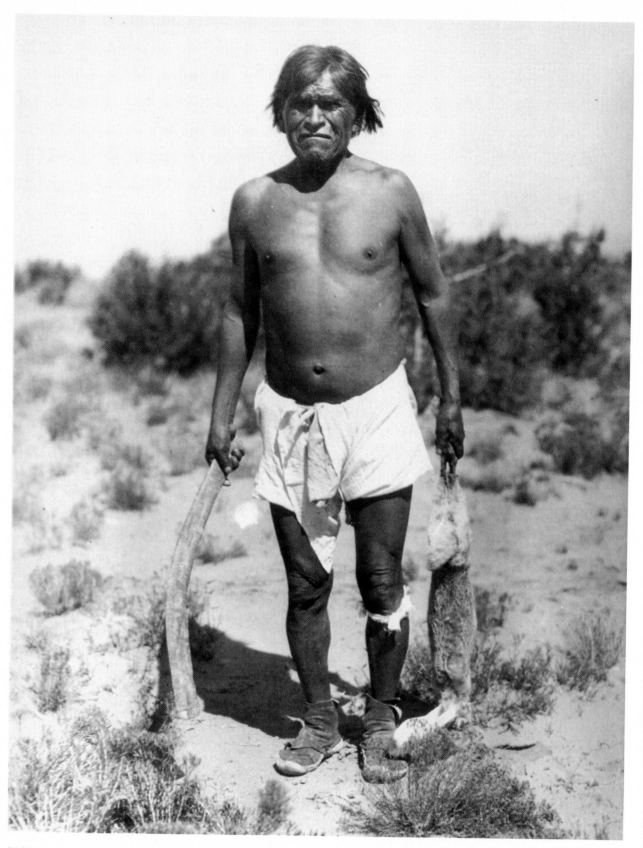

HOPI

A successful hunter holds his rabbit stick and prey. The black-tailed jack was part of the food supply of the Southwest, and despite its speed, could be brought down with an accurate throw of the curved stick.

O. C. Havens/1924.

POSSIBLY HOPI OR MEXICAN

A woman grinds corn meal on stone *metate*.
Despite the simplicity of the method, meal could be
ground in a variety of textures, depending
on kind of food to be prepared.

Bureau of Ameircan Ethnology/possibly Walpi Pueblo, Arizona/1895.

PAPAGO

The wheel was unknown
to Indian potters, who rolled clay
into ropes of required lengths,
and piled coils atop each other to desired
height and shape. The paddle beside potter
was used to shape and smooth the coils.

William Dinwiddie/Bureau of American Ethnology/
San Xavier Reservation, Arizona/1894.

SANTA CLARA

Woman ascending ladder with clay water
jug on her head. Dried peppers are hanging from
ladder rung, and squash are atop roof.

H. T. Cory/Bureau of Reclamation/Santa Clara Pueblo, New Mexico/1916.

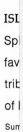

TLINGIT
Chief Shakes' house, at Wrangell,
Alaska, has three totem poles erected
around it and stilt bridge to reach
mainland during high water.

Possibly Lt. George T. Emmons, USN/1890s.

KWAKIUTL (Nimkish)

The legendary thunderbird carrying off
a whale is depicted on the side of an old house
at Alert Bay, British Columbia. Thunderbird,
a representation of the eagle, was
sacred and believed to produce thunder by
the beating of its wings, and lightning by the blinking
of its eyes. The design here probably was a crest of one
of the tribe's social groups. Vertical planks
are an indication of an old house.

Possibly C. O. Hastings/before 1889.

TLINGIT

Totem poles in front of Chief Kadashan's
house at Wrangell, Alaska. The eagle atop the lefthand
pole is the Kadashan family crest. The man-figure
surmounting the righthand pole is the Creator, and the raven
enfolding man in its wings (below) is the
Creator's grandson, who made mankind. The bottom
figure is a thunderbird. The carved figure at the
far left may be the bow of a canoe. The two-story
Euro-American house contrasts with old-style
structure at rear, made of planks and logs.

Photographer unknown/1883.

QUINAULT

Before the advent of Europeans, log canoes were made with stone tools after the interior was hollowed out by fire. Here man uses a metal adze to finish it. A roller eased the canoe into water.

TLINGIT (Sitka)

Interior of house at Sitka with a cooking fire in center of the floor. The partition on the platform at the rear screens an area for a pubescent girl or menstruating woman. Wall chests hold family possessions.

Photographer unknown/Alaska/1900-20.

KWAKIUTL
Village at Alert Bay, British Columbia, with totem and flag poles. The Canadians provided the flags. Strips drying on line at right probably are cedar bark— used for everything from fishing nets to ceremonial masks.

N. B. Miller/about 1888-89.

KAROK

Salmon fishing on Klamath River
in California, 1898. Fish were plucked
from rushing stream with a long-poled
plunge net by a man standing on a platform,
like that across river behind man
on left. A Karok Indian named Ichirie
(wearing basketry cap) carries load
of salmon in net sack with tumpline.

Photographer unknown/Katimin Rapids, Siskiyou County/1898.

ESKIMO (Aglegmiut)

Sod dwelling (right) and storehouse beside Naknek River,

Alaskan Peninsula, about 1890. To build a sod house, earth was excavated

to depth of several feet and a framework of posts and logs

erected. Grass and sod were piled on top. Women and children

lived in sod huts, but men and elder sons lived in ceremonial houses.

Storehouse might hold dried fish and seal and beaver fur for trade.

ESKIMO

Kow-ear-nuk wears winter boots of caribou hide with waterproof sealskin soles—strong, light, and warm. The three lines on her chin were tattooed at onset of menstruation and are a mark of adulthood. Behind her are salmon split for drying. Salmon fishing was a major Eskimo industry, the catch being used for winter rations and for sale to commercial fisheries started in Alaska in 1880s.

F. H. Nowell/Nome, Alaska/1906.

KOW-EAR-NUK

4076 A

CREE and CHIPEWYAN

A small girl with her birchbark basket
for gathering blueberries.

Francis Harper/mouth of Taltson
River, Mackenzie District, Northwest Territory/1914.

MAKAH

Lighthouse Jim's whaling gear
includes the harpoon and inflated
sealskin floats in
the boat. Whaling was a dangerous
and prestigious occupation,
and accompanied by rituals and
ceremonies to ensure whalers' protection.
The man who first harpooned the whale
could not eat it lest he be
unsuccessful in the future.

Asahel Curtis/1909.

INGALIK

Ice-fishing with woven willow trap in
Yukon River, near Anvik, Alaska. The ingenious
trap has vertical poles to submerge the rig and meshwork
to obstruct the fish and force them deeper,
into the funnel leading to the trap. The man has removed
small fish from his trap and holds short-handled
wooden scoop in left hand to enlarge hole.
Behind him are longer scoop and ice chisel.
Note delicacy of the sled design and
warm parka bundling small child.

John Wight Chapman/between Oct. and Feb., 1898.

ESKIMO (Kaniagmiut)

Eskimo on exhibition at Chicago's Columbian
Exposition of 1893 demonstrates a sinew-backed
bow and ivory-tipped arrow. He comes from Wood
Island, in the northeast Kodiak group of
southwestern Alaska, and wears ground-squirrel
skin coat. Squirrel skin is warm and
flexible and probably was used only
on special occasions.

Photographer unknown/Chicago, Illinois/1893.

CHOCTAW

Cane blowguns were used to hunt such animals as
squirrels, rabbits, and quail. Darts were usually
made of cane or pine and were 15 to 18 inches long.
The head was whittled to a fine point and the
tail was wrapped with cloth or tanned skin.
Joe Silestine demonstrates position for
shooting the blowgun.

Probably David I. Bushnell, Jr./
Bayou Lacomb, Louisiana/1908-09.

Preceding pages:

CHEROKEE

Not all Cherokee left the East when
they were ordered across the
Mississippi by President Andrew
Jackson. Those in North Carolina who refused
to go fled to the hills and hid. These are
probably some of their descendents. The
log cabin belongs to Ayunini, or Swimmer, the
man on the right. He was an important source
of information about Cherokee
history, mythology, medicine, and botany.

SEMINOLE

In Florida the Seminoles often built their houses,
known as chickees, high off the ground as
a protection against flooding. They were
open-sided with platform and thatched roof.

Frank A. Robinson/
Fort Lauderdale/about 1917.

James Mooney/Bureau of American Ethnology/
116   Qualla Reservation, North Carolina/1888.

Indians in the South were planting cotton long before it became king in the 1800s. The vast acreage needed for expanded production spurred whites to lease Catawba lands. By 1841 South Carolina had purchased all but one square mile. At the end of the 19th century about 600 acres were returned to the tribe. Here Emma Catney Brown hoes cotton on Cawtawba Reservation.

John R. Swanton/Bureau of American Ethnology/1918.

POOSEPATUCK

Tom Hill holds an eel spear at his boat landing at Mastic, Long Island. When fishing for eels, the iron rack in the center was positioned in the bow of a boat, filled with hay or rushes, and lit to attract the eels when they were surface-feeding at night. The decoys atop the shallow-draft boat appear to be manufactured, but early ones were made from bark and feathers. A net reel is at the left.

Francis Harper/1910.

CREE

Moose were the principal game sought by Cree. Here a man imitates their calls, using an old-style birch-bark device to amplify the sound. Moose were hunted best in the fall during the rut, which sets in with the first frost.

Edward S. Curtis/1926.

120

DAKOTA (Oglala)
Slow Bull enacts "Fire-Carrier Bringing
the Skull," a part of the Hunka
ceremony or Foster-parent Chant
performed by a man when he adopted
a child or wished to honor a friend.
Although this is probably a
posed picture done for the benefit of
Curtis who went West on his commission
from J.P. Morgan to Photograph
North American tribes. the Hunka
ceremony was practiced until the 1950s.

A Fool Dancer contemplatively smokes a clay pipe. Members of this Society acted as "contraries" during their two- to four-hour ceremony, executing actions in reverse order (such as riding horses backwards or bathing in a river after drying themselves) and saying the opposite of what they meant. The Fool Dance was one of the few Northern Plains masked dances.

Sumner W. Matteson/Fort Belknap Reservation, Montana/1906.

ASSINIBOIN

The Sun Dance was officially discouraged, and in some places prohibited, after the 1880s. But because it was combined with July 4th celebrations, it was allowed on the Fort Belknap Reservation in Montana. A Sun Dancer is receiving gifts, probably including the horse at the left. His body paint, the feather in his hair, his kilt, and the eagle-bone whistle around his neck are all part of the traditional costume for the ceremony. Note, however, that his hair is cut in a white style.

Sumner W. Matteson/1906.

ASSINIBOIN

Two Boys (right), leader of the Fool Dancers, and one of his helpers. His mask and costume are made of canvas, the latter patterned after a woman's fringed dress. He carries a rattle-staff hung with dew claws of deer and has a bone whistle in his mouth.

BLACKFOOT (Piegan)

Spotted Eagle, Chief Elk, and Bull Child blow eagle-bone whistles as part of a Sun Dance ritual to insure good weather during the ceremony. Bull Child wears a traditional wreath of juniper or sage; Chief Elk has a plume hanging from the little finger of each hand. They are inside the medicine lodge, erected for the occasion. In the background is a bough-covered booth, on the west side of the lodge, where they stay when not dancing.

Sumner W. Matteson/Fort Belknap Reservation, Montana/1906.

Photographer unknown/about 1900.

BLACKFOOT (Blood)

Owns the Paint, or Takes Paint,
fulfills a vow by undergoing
self-torture during the Sun Dance.
A skewer, hooked through his chest
muscles, is attached to rope
tied high on center pole.
He is pulling back to
rip himself free. His body is
painted white and he has
sage grass around his wrists,
ankles, and head. As part
of the ritual, he blows on an
eagle-bone whistle
and stares at center pole.

R. N. Wilson/Alberta, Canada/1892. (Courtesy
American Museum of Natural History, New York.)

A Zuñi eagle cage.

Hillers, photo.

ZUNI

Young eagles, captured from their nests, were kept in cages, such as this one made of adobe and stakes, for their plumage, which was highly valued for ceremonial purposes. Zuni both collected the molt and plucked the birds. Tail feathers were especially prized for masks and rattles, and were worn during such occasions as the Flute Ceremony.

John K. Hillers/Bureau of American Ethnology/Zuni Pueblo, New Mexico/1879.

ZUNI

Members such as these of the Newekwe, or Galaxy Fraternity, were tribal shamans who cared for the sick. Most of their cures were affected through magic. The cured were then initiated into the society.

Matilda Coxe Stevenson/Zuni Pueblo/New Mexico/around 1909.

HOPI (Walpi)

The man and youth are impersonating hehea kachinas—supernatural beings—during the Powamu, or bean-planting, Ceremony. It was hoped that the earth would be purified or renovated for future planting, but the main purpose was to celebrate the return of the Kachinas.

James Mooney/Bureau of American Ethnology/Walpi Pueblo, Arizona/1893.

HOPI

The Flute Ceremony was held on alternate
years with the Snake Dance for rain, sun,
and the propagation of the corn crop. This
is most likely a preliminary ritual to
the Flute Ceremony held at a spring where
they drew their drinking water. Some of
the priests are wearing emblems on
their back representing the sun.

Possibly George A. Dorsey/Field Columbian Museum/before 1905.

HOPI

The Flute Ceremony lasted nine days
and culminated in a public dance. This
may be a preliminary ritual, possibly the
arrival of the priests outside the
pueblo before the dance.

Possibly George A. Dorsey/Field Columbian
Museum/before 1905. 135

APACHE (Mescalero)

Four masked Mountain Spirits, or Gan Dancers, represent benevolent spirits and are dancing

evil ones away. They are believed to represent the four cardinal points of the universe.

Bows and arrows were unusual in the rite and suggest that this event involved ''war medicine.''

Photographer unknown/possibly at San Carlo Agency/New Mexico/1899.

SANTO DOMINGO

The dancer on the right is probably a member of the Squash Kiva. Every Indian in the pueblo belongs to one or two kivas, or ceremonial groups, the Squash or Turquoise Kiva. The boy on the right is a participant in the Corn Dance.

Adam Clark Vroman/Santo Domingo Pueblo, New Mexico/1899.

HUPA

Boat Dance was part of the White Deerskin Dance
held in late summer to ensure abundance the following
year and to appease the spirits. Canoes were made
of hollowed-out redwood logs by the Yurok, a tribe
to the north. Men took the occasion to display
such prized possessions as obsidian knives and albino
deerskins decorated with woodpecker crowns.

Photographer unknown/Trinity River, Hoopa Valley,
California/before 1898.

Preceding pages: SANTA CLARA

The Corn Dance in progress. A participant
in the dance was trained from childhood, and
it was his tribal obligation to participate in
the dance whenever it was held.

Matilda Coxe Stevenson/Santa Clara Pueblo,
New Mexico/December, 1911.

SIA

Boy on the stool is being treated for
illness by five shamans in a ceremonial chamber
of the Giant Society. The men, seated behind
a row of fetishes, holding plumes and straws
in the left hand and rattles in the right,
utter chants to exorcise the disease. The
white line separating the boy from
the men is corn meal.

Matilda Coxe Stevenson/Sia Pueblo, New Mexico/1888-89. 141

KWAKIUTL (Koskimo) Copper "shields" were wealth and prestige to many tribes along the Northwest Coast. These are members of the secret Hamatsa Society at a winter ceremonial feast after the purchase of a shield. Winter was a sacred season among the Kwakiutl; it was a time when supernatural powers were believed to be nearby. The men wear cedar-bark neck- and head-rings, and some of the women wear blankets decorated with mother-of-pearl buttons, used only for ceremonial occasions.

C. O. Hastings or Franz Boaz/Fort Rupert, Vancouver Island, British Columbia, 1894.

DUWAMISH

"Lifting over the daylight," as it was
called, was part of the Spirit Canoe Ceremony
reenacted to recover the lost soul of a dead
patient. The ritual depicted journey of the
shamans to land of the dead to recover the body.

J. D. Leechman/Tolt, King County, Washington/1920.

THOMPSON

Burial practices varied from tribe to tribe. The Thompson of the Northwest Coast buried their dead in the ground, but the Crow of the western Plains placed theirs in trees. Baskets and pots were placed by the Thompson near the deceased so they could take them on journey to the land of the dead.

Richard Maynard/Thompson River, British Columbia/about 1875.

ARAPAHO

The Ghost Dance continued
to be practiced on a few reservations
after the massacre of Big Foot's band at Wounded
Knee. Photographer Mooney called this picture,
taken three years later, "Inspiration."
Women are chanting in a trance-like state.

James Mooney/Bureau of American Ethnology/
146   Oklahoma Territory/about 1893.

ARAPAHO

Mooney called this picture of the Ghost Dance ''Praying.'' Before Wounded Knee, participants wore shirts painted with magic designs to make them bulletproof, but after the massacre Indians lost faith in their efficacy.

James Mooney/Bureau of American Ethnology/ Oklahoma Territory/about 1893. **147**

For the past one hundred and sixty-seven years, the United States Government has brought Indians to Washington, D.C., primarily to convince them to part with their land, needed for settlers, cotton planters, miners, cattlemen, farmers, and for dams, railroads, highways, power plants, oil wells, and now pipelines. Over the years, Indians have come to the capital hoping to regain the land of which they were once so much a part, and seeking Government assurance that it would abide by its treaty obligations.

Jefferson, the first President to bring Indians to Washington, continued the colonial policy of forcing them from their lands. Concerned with acquiring territory for the new Nation, he bought from France, in 1803, all of the land between the Mississippi River and the Rocky Mountains. He then deported the Shawnee and Miami from the Old Northwest, and the Choctaw from central Mississippi, across the great river to the eastern part of the Louisiana Purchase, which the Government set aside as Indian Territory.

Tatschaga, a leader of the Osage, who once occupied vast stretches of grassland west of the Mississippi, was summoned to Washington in 1806 and subsequently taken on a tour of the East. Addressing the senate chamber of Massachusetts that year, he said, "Our complexions differ from yours, but our hearts are the same color, and you ought to love us, for we are the original and true Americans." The immigrant Americans did not, however, love them, and two years later took by treaty all Osage land between the Missouri and Arkansas rivers.

The Government, more interested in Indian land than in the Indians, recorded very few images of the red men who came to Washington until 1821, when Charles Bird King was commissioned to paint the portraits of the most famous Indian chiefs.

He painted the Indians in the full splendor of their authentic costumes and idealized their natural dignity. Many of the pictures were subsequently published in a collection called *History of the Indian Tribes of North America, with Biographical Sketches and Anecdotes of the Principal Chiefs, 1836-44.* Thomas McKenney, who had been head of the Indian Bureau of the War Department from 1824 to 1830, and James Hall, a western enthusiast, supplied the text.

Photographs of Indians in Washington began about fifteen years after King's portraits left off. The camera, instead of idealizing them, portrayed them with abrasive social realism and caught moments between their ebbing ways and the floodtide of Manifest Destiny.

Alexander Gardner was one of the earliest Washington photographers to take Indian pictures. He came to the capital in the 1850s and opened his own studio in 1863 at Seventh and D streets. During the last year of the Civil War he became a semi-official Government photographer, assisting Mathew Brady with his remarkable pictures of the Army of the Potomac. When Indians came to the capital it was only natural, through his Government connections, that Gardner should photograph them.

Mrs. Gardner kept what she called "a smelly collection" of Indian clothes in which to dress the Indians for their pictures, because she thought they looked too scruffy in their own clothes after many weeks of travel. Other photographers, such as A. Zeno Shindler and C. M. Bell, did the same, and some pictures consequently have members of the same or different tribes wearing the same shirts or holding the same tobacco pouches.

Indian delegations came by train, usually in groups of two to twenty, and were accompanied by an agent. The official lodg-

Preceding pages:
APACHE (Chiricahua)
Geronimo and some of
his band after they were taken
prisoner for the final time in 1886.
They have stopped along
the Southern Pacific Railroad
line in Texas, and Geronimo sits
third from the right in
the front row. The
Chiricahua had been assigned
earlier to White Mountain
Reservation in the
Arizona Territory, but the famous
chief and his followers
fled to Mexico, from
where they carried out fierce raids.
They had just surrendered
when this picture was taken and
were on their way to Florida
to join, as they
thought, their wives. When they
arrived, however,
they were imprisoned in Fort
Pickens. Arrests, removals,
and relocations such as this often
were the subject of
Indians' complaints on their
visits to Washington.
A. J. McDonald/near Nueces River, Texas/1886.

ing for the visiting tribes was Ben Beveridge's Inn on Third Street. The Department of the Interior, created in 1849, covered their expenses and sometimes had to reimburse Beveridge for alleged damages.

Bringing the Indians to Washington was a diplomatic coup for the Government, because all who came were overawed by evidence of its wealth and power, and by the large crowds of white people. No matter how hostile the Indians might have been upon arrival, few returned home to lead a war party against the Government.

The visitors were given presents of suits, boots, military jackets, powder horns, silver-plated rifles, peace medals, and American flags to take home with them to insure their continued good will toward the expanding Nation.

Silver peace medals were highly prized and often bestowed upon the wearer the status of chief. They had the image of the incumbent President minted on the front, and some had the war-emblem eagle on the back. Until 1812 the medals were symbols of allegiance to the new government; after the final British defeat they were given for promises of good behavior; and after 1880, when all the good behavior necessary for the purposes of the Nation had been extracted and most of the Indians were on reservations, they were awarded as first prize in livestock shows.

The Indians of the Great Plains came to Washington more frequently than any other group, because passage through their land was needed for all travel west of the Mississippi. They also had the most land to give up. Besides Plains Indians, former eastern tribes, living in the Indian Territory of the Great Plains since the 1830s, often came to seek protection against the tribes on whose land they had been resettled.

Eventually, the Bureau of American Ethnology, created in 1879 by John Wesley Powell, became the repository of Indian photographs. John K. Hillers, who had accompanied Major Powell on his early Colorado River expeditions, became the Bureau's first official photographer.

Some Indians came to Washington at the request of the Bureau, whose members wanted to study their customs and languages. Some of the photographs were a result of such researches, and each was taken against a plain backdrop, instead of the artificial rocks and painted screens that studio photographers had used in the sixties.

The Indians of the Arctic, Subarctic, and Northwest Coast are not represented in this section because much of their land was under the jurisdiction of the Canadian government, and because the United States did not become interested in Alaskan land until petroleum was discovered in the 1960s. Today, Alaskan Indian and Eskimo representatives are coming to Washington to fight for their ancestral lands as did the Plains Indians a century ago.

One of the first Indians to be photographed in Washington was John Ross. He came to the capital in 1858 on behalf of the Cherokee, who had been exiled to Indian Territory some twenty years before. Ross sought Government protection against the Kiowas and Comanches, fierce tribes of the central Plains, against whom the Government had promised aid in return for Cherokee land in Georgia. Ross's trip was only one of many he made between 1831, when he pleaded the rights of his people to their land before the Supreme Court, and 1866, when he died in Washington, still trying to procure protection for his people.

What happened to the Cherokee and the other four Civilized Tribes—as they were called—in the Southeast during the

1830s foreshadowed what was to befall the rest of the Indians by the 1890s. White settlers in the twenties coveted the rich farm lands of the Cherokee, extending from South Carolina through Georgia, for their cotton plantations. The cotton gin, invented in 1793, had suddenly made wider-scale planting feasible by its ability to separate seeds from fibers. Consequently, white planters wanted the Cherokee lands.

When the Georgia legislature decided that Indian lands belonged to whites, Ross appealed the ruling to the Supreme Court. Although Chief Justice John Marshall upheld the Cherokee appeal, President Jackson overruled it and proclaimed that the will of the state legislature should be the law of the land. Jackson carried the policy of Indian removal advocated by Jefferson to its extreme. In 1830 an act of Congress ordered the Five Civilized Tribes off their lands and deported them to Indian Territory. The newly-created First Dragoons oversaw their exodus, beginning in 1832, and many an Indian went on his thousand-mile journey through the wilderness on foot.

In 1857, the year the first photographs of Indian delegations were taken, the Plains Indians west of the Mississippi, except for those in Indian Territory, had few complaints against the whites. Although gold had been discovered nine years before in California, the great surge of westward migration did not really begin until after the Civil War. Railroads had not yet crossed Indian lands, the discovery of minerals had not pushed them far from their homes, the buffalo still roamed, and farmers' plows had not turned under the sacred earth.

Most of the photographs of the red men in Washington were taken after the Civil War, as their grievances against the whites mounted and the Government launched an all-out program of land appropriation.

Until Ulysses S. Grant became President there had been no explicit Government policy regarding the Indians west of the Mississippi. Leaders had not been bent on removing them altogether because they considered the Great Plains to be the Great American Desert, fit only for sage grass, buffalo, and prairie dogs.

In 1870, the year Grant came to office, the Indian Bureau was rampant with corruption and inefficiency. In an effort to ameliorate conditions on reservations Grant instituted what is known as the Quaker Policy, which advocated that missionaries be agents. Supposedly, they would be above corruption and more humane toward their charges. In addition, a Peace Policy was established which sought to further assimilate reservation Indians into American society by treating them with kindness.

These benevolent policies may have been adopted by missionaries but they were not adopted by the Army. In 1871 a series of bloody slaughters, known as the Plains Wars, began. No longer was it necessary to conclude treaties to secure Indian lands. The red men were considered wards of the Government and their land belonged to the Nation. This provided the rationale for accelerating the reservation system. Indians were sent to reserves so their rights to the land would be "reserved" for them and protected by Government agents.

The reservation system grew out of the agency system, established by the Second Articles of Confederation in 1786, and was based on the notion that settlers had the right of dominion merely through their arrival. Early colonists expelled the Indians from the eastern shores, following what they considered their predestined course because they had been elected by God to settle there. This principle of might making the right hand of God pushed the frontier across the Nation and, en route, the Indians into reservations.

The Articles of Confederation guaranteed the land west of the Appalachian Mountains to the Indians in perpetuity and divided the region in two sections at the Ohio River, each to be administered by a bonded agent appointed by the President. By that time, pioneers had only reached the foothills of the range.

The land of the Ute is a good example of what happened to many tribes west of the Mississippi. Theirs was the high, dry land of eastern Utah and central and western Colorado, extending down into New Mexico. Although they lived mostly in the Uintah Mountains, some bands dwelt in the San Juan Mountains east of the Great Divide and occasionally descended to the Plains to hunt buffalo.

After the Mexican War, the Ute came under the jurisdiction of the United States according to the terms of the Treaty of Guadalupe-Hidalgo. In 1851 the Government held a council with the Ute, who vowed perpetual peace and granted free passage to travelers and the establishment of forts, trading posts, and agencies in their land. By the treaty, the United States prepared the legal way for the Government to expropriate Ute land by promising to "adjust their territorial boundaries...as the government of said States may deem conducive to the happiness and prosperity of said Indians."

What the poor land lacked in wildlife, the earth made up in minerals. The red men, who dug for succulent roots, gathered pinyon nuts and berries, and hunted small animals for food, were quickly pushed out when American miners found gold in the Rockies in 1858. The population of the area grew so fast that Colorado became a territory three years later.

By 1863, conflicts between Ute and prospectors were so severe that the Government made a treaty with the Tabeguache band under which the Indians surrendered a million acres and all mineral rights and were confined to the mountains south of the headwaters of the Colorado River. In return for their lands and for railroad rights through their reservations, the Government promised the Ute five stallions, some cattle and sheep, and $20,000 annually in provisions for ten years. It is a matter of record that the United States failed to keep its promises except for the taking of the land.

By 1868, all Ute were on reservations. In the preceding decade, $25 million worth of gold had been extracted from mines in Colorado on what had once been their land.

Major Powell, appointed special commissioner by the Indian Bureau, investigated Ute and Paiute conditions in 1873 and used John Hiller's photographs to publicize the plight of the Indians. For his time, Powell took an extremely enlightened position. Although he believed that the Indians should definitely be confined to reservations, he maintained that the land reserves should no longer be, in his words, a "pen where a horde of savages are to be fed with flour and beef, to be supplied with blankets from the government bounty, and to be furnished with paints and geegaws by the greed of traders, but that a reservation should be a school of industry and a home for these unfortunate people."

Gold and silver influenced the route of the first transcontinental railroad. Construction was begun on the Union Pacific and Central Pacific in 1865, just when the mines of the Comstock Lode in Nevada had reached peak production. When completed the railroad went directly through the area into California and, along the way, through the land of the Paiute. The Government never made any formal agreements with them for the right of way, but it did grant the railroad twenty square miles of land for each mile of track laid. By 1871, the Government had given the railroads 180 million acres throughout the West, virtually all of it formerly occupied by, or considered the ancestral lands of, Indians.

The iron horse carried settlers across the country from Council Bluffs to Sacramento in a matter of days whereas, in previous years, the same trip by covered wagon over the old California Trail had taken months. Furthermore, the railroads sold their grant lands to the newcomers for $2.50 to $20 an acre. In the 1870s they took miners to Colorado and Nevada, and hide-hunters and mule-skinners to the Great Plains for buffalo skins that would fetch up to $3.50 apiece back east. The railroads transported cattle to Chicago from Abilene and Dodge City after long drives up from Texas on the Chisholm and Western trails. And finally, when the buffalo were gone, the railroads brought in farmers, who turned what had once been dusty prairies of blue-stem and buffalo grass into vast wheat and corn fields.

Gold became the pathfinder for the Army when it was discovered in the Black Hills of South Dakota in 1872. It seemed, at the time, of little consequence that the land was sacred to the Dakota and had been reserved for them by treaty four years before. Custer, known to the Indians by the name of "Long Hair," and his Seventh Cavalry followed the prospectors into the hills to confirm their reports and to take care of any opposition to their presence along the way. Although he and his two hundred fifty men suffered a permanent set back at Little Bighorn on June 25, 1876, the remaining Seventh Cavalry pressed on and by 1877 terminated much of the trouble

with the Dakota.

By 1890 all of the Indians of the Great Plains who had survived Civil War veteran General William Tecumseh Sherman's policy that "all who cling to their old hunting ground are hostile and will remain so until killed off" were confined to reservations. With their source of food, clothing, and shelter gone, they were dealt Government rations: one pair of wool pants and a jacket per man, a flannel skirt and 24 yards of cotton per woman, one pound of meat and one pound of flour per day, and canvas for their tepees. These supplies proved too generous and expensive for the Government and, in some cases, were terminated. Instead, cash payments of approximately $2 per person a year were substituted.

Once the Indians were on reservations the Government was eager for them to take up farming. Crops required still less land than hunting and the produce would save the Government further aid. The Dawes Allotment Act of 1887 attempted to coerce Indians into becoming farmers by offering one hundred and sixty acres to the head of each family and forty additional acres for each child.

The act had two purposes. The first was to break up the reservations and the tribal structure of Indian society. With a farm, it was believed, each man would become his own master. It was also designed to give more land to the whites: whatever was left over from the allotment was to be sold to white settlers. The Board of Indian Commissions said the act was designed so that the Indian would "be lifted up out of his barbarism into self-supporting Christian citizenship."

The act did not cause the Indians to give up their ways or their tribal structure, but it did deplete their holdings from 138 million acres to 48 million acres.

Petalashero, the younger, or Man Chief, wears his bear-claw necklace and otter-fur turban and holds a catlinite pipe, often a symbol of peace. It is not known what brought him to Washington in 1858. By that time his tribe's numbers had diminished greatly because of disease introduced by whites. The Pawnee lived along the Platte River, which westward-bound settlers followed across country along the Oregon Trail, and were one of the first Plains tribes to feel the impact of Manifest Destiny.

Probably Julian Vannerson in James E. McClees' studio/Washington, D.C./1858.

CHEROKEE

By 1858, John Ross had made many trips to
Washington on behalf of his people. He had
sought unsuccessfully to retain the tribe's
rights to its land in Georgia; and after
it was removed to Indian Territory, in what
is now Oklahoma, he tried unremittingly to
get the Government to keep its promise
to protect it from neighboring Plains tribes.

A. Zeno Shindler/Washington, D.C./1858.

DAKOTA (Oglala)

Red Cloud was one of the few leaders to win a military campaign against the U.S. Army. The treaty of 1868 that ended the Red Cloud War asked for no concessions on the part of the Dakota, only peace. The Oglala forfeited no land, and Red Cloud refused to sign the document until Army forts in Dakota hunting grounds were removed. As a result the United States abandoned those along the Bozeman Trail. Red cloud first came to Washington in 1870, and thereafter made at least ten trips to the capital, the last in 1897.

C. M. Bell/Washington, D.C./1880.

IROQUOIS (Seneca)

Ely Samuel Parker served in the Civil War
and became a personal friend of and military
secretary to General Grant. Parker resigned
from the Army in 1869, and Grant, then President,
appointed him head of the Bureau of Indian Affairs.

Photographer not recorded/about 1867.

KANSA

At the time Pi-Sing was in Washington, the Kansa were in destitute
condition on their reservation, which they could not leave to hunt
for fear of Cheyenne with whom they were in constant conflict. In
1868 the Government had distributed only limited goods to prevent
starvation but had not paid the annuities for that year.

By A. Zeno Shindler, Washington, D.C., 1868.

DAKOTA (Brule Band)

Spotted Tail's wife is wearing a heavily
beaded yoke which was a new style of Plains
dress at the time. Spotted Tail surrendered
to the U. S. Army in 1855 for his part in
the slaughter of an Army unit
the year before. Eventually
Spotted Tail gained favor with the
Government, and he was killed by Indians
in the eighties for being a collaborator.

Alexander Gardner/Washington, D.C./1872.

Five Sauk & Fox and three Kansa flank the U. S. Commissioner of Indian
Affairs (standing) and the chief clerk of the Indian Bureau. The Sauk
& Fox had just signed a treaty ceding all their remaining land in
Kansas for $1 per acre. In return they were to get a reservation
in Indian Territory, a school building, a teacher, a doctor, and a blacksmith.

Alexander Gardner/Washington, D.C./February, 1867.

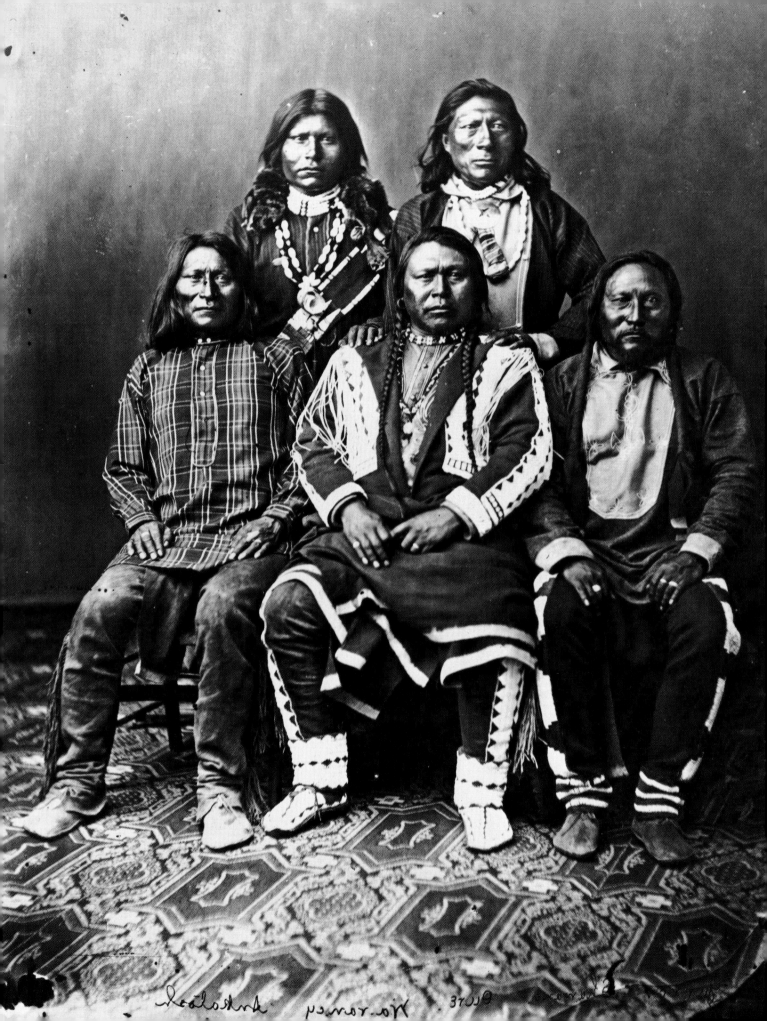

ZUNI

Wewha, a male transsexual, wears typical Zuni female attire: a dress of cotton cloth embroidered on top, a woven belt, and a silver necklace. Her hair—transsexuals were referred to by their assumed gender—is in a woman's style: short, with bangs and a queue down the back wrapped with yarn or cloth. The choice of an opposite role was a final decision made at puberty. Women might joke about the situation, but were inclined to regard her with favor because she remained in the household and worked harder than they did.

UTE

Ute leaders came to Washington in 1868 to discuss the creation of two reservations, the Colorado and Uintah reserves, and the cession of large areas of land in Colorado and Utah. Gold had been discovered on Ute land in 1858, and miners were encroaching upon the territory. Ouray, chief of the Umcompahgre band, is seated in the center.

Photographed in William G. Chamberlin Studio/ Denver, Colordo/1868-72.

John K. Hillers/Bureau of American Ethnology/Washington, D.C./1884-87.

CHIPPEWA (Leech Lake Band)

One Called From A Distance wears a cloth
and beaded turban, a porcupine-hair roach, a beaded
yoke with typical floral design, and a beaded
bandolier bag across chest. His tomahawk has both
bowl of a pipe and spontoon blade typical
of 17th and 18th century European half-pike.

Bureau of American Ethnology/Washington, D.C./1894.

CREEK

Hotalke Yahola wears a silver headband,
a crescent-shaped gorget, and a beaded sash.

DeLancey Gill/Bureau of American Ethnology/Washington, D.C. 1903.

CHEYENNE (Southern)

Little Chief, or Magpie Eagle Feathers,
wears a Benjamin Harrison Peace
Medal issued in 1889.

William Dinwiddie/Bureau of American
Ethnology/Washington, D.C./1895.

MISSOURI

Prairie Turtle wearing a yarn turban,
metal ball-and-cone earrings, and necklaces.

John K. Hillers/Bureau of American Ethnology/Washington, D.C./before 1894.

Preceding pages: ARAPAHO and CHEYENNE
Delegations outside the Arts & Industries Building
of Smithsonian Institution in 1899. Third from the right
in the front row is Little Chief, who also appears
on page 176. Third from left in middle row is Andrew
John, a Seneca who conducted Indian groups to
Smithsonian to be photographed at $1 per man.

CHIPPEWA (Red Lake Band)

Indians traveling to capital usually brought festive or ceremonial costumes with them for special occasions, otherwise wore mixed or non-Indian clothing. These Chippewa posed in partial costume (opposite), perhaps borrowing some items from stock photographer had on hand, and then in white man's "civvies" (above).

DeLancey Gill/Bureau of American Ethnology/Washington, D.C./1901. **181**

NEZ PERCE

Chief Joseph at 61, four years before his death. Though wearing
a feathered war bonnet, he is remembered as a man of peace and wisdom
who won respect and admiration for his patient and persistent efforts
to save his ancestral land—the Wallowa Valley in Oregon—from
white encroachment. His efforts ended in tragedy, however, when the
Nez Perce were pursued in 1877 by American soldiers and
volunteers in the course of a 1500-mile trek to reach sanctuary
in Canada. After a five-day battle the vanquished leader surrendered
to General Nelson A. Miles, saying, "Hear me, my chiefs, I am
tired; my heart is sick and sad. From where the sun now stands I will
fight no more forever." Chief Joseph survived the ordeal but many
of his people did not. He came to Washington many times afterward to
urge the Government to let his people return to their
homeland as had been promised upon their defeat. By 1883 his efforts
and public sympathy pressured the Government into permitting some of the
Nez Perce to relocate on the Lapwai Reservation in Idaho, and finally
on the Colville Reservation in Washington. Chief Joseph was never allowed
to return to his Wallowa Valley to live, although he visited it several
times. He died on the Colville Reservation in 1904. Among many notable
statements on behalf of all Indians, he said:
"If the white man wants to live in peace with the Indian he can
live in peace. . . . Treat all men alike. Give them all the same
law. Give them all an even chance to live and grow. All men
were made by the same Great Spirit Chief. They are all brothers.
The earth is the mother of all people, and all people
should have equal rights upon it."

DeLancey Gill/Bureau of American Ethnology, Washington, D.C./1900.

EPILOGUE

Members of the Seventh Cavalry who
participated in the massacre
at Wounded Knee, December 29, 1890.

Indians have suffered at the hand of the United States Government most of the injustices suffered by the colonists under the sceptre of George the Third and expressed so vehemently on July 4, 1776.

Since 1786, when the Indian agency system was established under the Articles of Confederation, the Federal Government has "obstructed the Administration of Justice... erected a Multitude of New Offices, and sent hither Swarms of Officers to harrass" the Indians, "kept among" them, "in Times of Peace, Standing Armies, without the[ir] consent," subjected them "to a Jurisdiction foreign to their" ways, deprived them "in many Cases, of the Benefits of Trial by Jury," and completed "the Works of Death, Desolation, and Tyranny, already begun with circumstances of Cruelty and Perfidy, scarcely paralleled in the most barbarous Ages, and totally unworthy... of a civilized nation."

Not only did the Declaration of Independence set forth the grievances of the colonists against the Crown, but it also established, by implication, what was to become official Indian policy by describing them as "Inhabitants of our Frontiers, the merciless Indian Savages, whose known Rule of Warfare, is undistinguished Destruction, of all Ages, Sexes and Conditions."

Ever more merciless, the United States Government had spent $2 million by 1890 for killing each Indian, according to some of its own reports. In Plains Wars of the seventies alone, it spent $1 million per Indian. Legions were wiped out, not only by the misfortunes of battle, protecting lands and homes, but also by epidemics of smallpox and malaria introduced sometimes by settlers and sometimes by army men. When the Government decided during the Plains Wars of the 1870s that the red menace could not be wiped out by force because it was too costly, it undertook to have the Indians absorbed into the mainstream of American life.

One of the alleged purposes of the reservation system was to induce the Indians to give up their ways, so they could share in the American Dream for which they had already given up their land. To this end they were educated by white teachers in English, indoctrinated by missionaries in Christianity, taught manual skills and farming techniques and, finally, in 1924, were made citizens of the United States. Nonetheless, they did not abandon their culture and were not assimilated into the middle-class melting pot.

In 1928, the Merriam Report admitted that assimilation and the attempt to annihilate Indian culture had been a total failure. Indians were among the poorest of the poor, lived on impoverished lands, had an average annual income of $100 per person, lacked medical facilities, and suffered acutely from disease and malnutrition. The average life span was forty-four years.

As part of the New Deal program to revitalize the country during the Depression, President Franklin D. Roosevelt appointed John Collier head of the Bureau of Indian Affairs, with a mandate to rectify the desperate situation. Collier saw to it that tribal cultures were recognized as a positive influence and undertook to strengthen the Indian heritage. The tribes were allowed to hold their hallowed ceremonies, arts and crafts were promoted, and schools were set up that taught subjects in tribal languages.

In 1934 Congress passed the Wheeler-Howard Act, which stressed tribal self-government and economic self-sufficiency, prohibited all further division of tribal lands, and returned surpluses not in use by whites to the Indians. No matter how well-intentioned the land policy was, it came too late. Of the 90 million acres lost by the Indians to the Government after 1890 only three million were restored.

The 1950s brought an end to the enlightened policies of the Government toward the Indians. As part of a national program of reduced Government spending, Congress introduced termination programs designed to cut off all Federal aid to the tribes.

In many instances, termination proved to be disastrous. One of the tribes subjected to the economies of the fifties was the Menominee of Wisconsin. Prior to termination in 1961, the Government had helped the tribe and had employed whites to run a highly profitable lumber mill without teaching the Indians how to operate it. Consequently, when all Federal aid to the Menominee was cut off, the tribe was in no way prepared for the rough-and-tumble of rugged individualism. The tribe plummeted from a community with $10 million in cash assets to the squalor of bankruptcy. Production was curtailed, unemployment rose, and the hospital closed. To meet its debts, the tribe was forced to sell off much of its valuable land, which was located in the middle of Wisconsin's most coveted timber area, to land developers. In 1970, fourteen percent of the people were on welfare.

Termination proved so disastrous, and the shame of it spread so far, that the policy was eventually modified. Currently, the Government espouses self-determination. It seems to be a minimal program that admits, on the one hand, the right of the Indians to their tribal heritage, and operates a few Federally-funded programs. On the other hand, it has not gone so far as to recognize the validity of groups which maintain that the Government should meet its old treaty obligations and uphold what is commonly called an honorable peace.

Today the Indians, after having given

up their country, are in no man's land. They do not even enjoy the status afforded a defeated enemy that has, in the past, received millions of dollars in postwar rehabilitation aid.

When a Red Power group exercised its right to self-determination in 1969 by taking over the abandoned island of Alcatraz to establish a cultural center, under a clause in a Sioux treaty of 1868 stipulating that unused lands should revert to Indians, the Government ordered the electricity and water cut off and forced its surrender.

One of the demands of Indian groups is that the Government cease expropriating, once and for all, their land. A super-highway was built in the 1960s directly through the Seneca Reservation in New York State, and today history may repeat itself if the Alaska pipeline is constructed. It may do in the 1980s to the caribou herds and Eskimos what railroads did to the buffalo herds and Plains Indians a century ago.

The Eskimo and Aleut have given up 400 million acres to oil interests. Some whites say that they are being adequately reimbursed, for all those who have at least one-quarter Eskimo or Aleut blood will share in a payment of $962,500,000 and have been allowed to keep 40 million acres. Others, however, hold that money will never make up for the completeness of Arctic life that will inevitably and quickly pass.

Most Indians, of whatever tribe, today want the prerogative of remaining Indian and not joining white middle-class society. This does not mean that the Indians want to be poor, but unfortunately it is the price they have been forced to pay white men for being red men and for preserving their heritage. Nevertheless, the question remains: What inalienable rights do the Indians have to determine their lives.

Wounded Knee, May 7, 1973.
A burial service outside the church for
Indian killed by a sniper.

A participant in the takeover of the
Bureau of Indian Affairs in
Washington, D.C., November, 1972.

Frank Johnston/The Washington Post.

Numbers assigned by the Bureau of American Ethnology and National Anthropological Archives to photographs in the collection of the Smithsonian Institution. An asterisk (*) indicates an original negative.

Frontispiece, 3253-B*; p. 10, 4660*; p. 22, 55,752; p. 23, 43,196; p. 24, 3418*; p. 25, 1190-B*; p. 26, 1535*; p. 28, T 15,904*; p. 29, 3195-A; p. 30, 56,831; p. 31, 56,388; p. 32, 56,889; p. 33, 47,999; p. 34, 2880-C-7*; p. 35, 2975-G-1*; p. 36 left, 56,961; p. 36 right, 56,802; p. 37, 56,770; p. 38 left, 2629*; p. 38 right, 2580-B-8; p. 39 left, 4265-A-1*; p. 39 right, 4516*; p. 40, 45,987-C; p. 41, 2815-4*; p. 42, 53,507; p. 43, 2412*; p. 44, 2145*; p. 45 top, 2429*; p. 45 bottom, 1837-A; p. 46 left, 53,599; p. 46 right, 53,599-A; p. 47, 56,960; p. 48, 43,219; p. 49 left, 56,803; p. 49 right, 56,769; p. 50, SI 3862*; p. 51, HBC 348,859:(4)*; p. 52, 56,715; p. 54, 858*; p. 55, 44,262-E; p. 56, 53,887; p. 57, 1044-A*; p. 58, 897*; p. 60, 617; p. 61, 836; p. 62, 43,118-A; p. 73, 34,055-A; p. 74, 215-H; p. 75, 53,401-A; p. 76, 55,928; p. 77 top, 56,375; p. 77 bottom, 1245-B*; p. 78, 720-C; p. 80, 1754-A-2*; p. 81, 4644*; p. 82, 54,510; p. 84, 4606*; p. 85, 2890-B-34*; p. 86, 1633*; p. 87, 4276-A-1*; p. 88, 2227-B*; p. 90, 2267-J*; p. 91, 4524*; p. 92, 2267-A*; p. 94, 4742*; p. 95, 1838*; p. 96, 2755-B*; p. 97, 4566*; p. 98, 56,955; p. 99 top, 56,888; p. 99 bottom, 4548*; p. 100, 56,764; p. 102, 49,486; p. 103, 14,838-C; p. 104 top, 56,965; p. 104 bottom, 56,768; p. 105, 56,438; p. 106, 56,749; p. 108, 33,370; p. 109, 46,736-H; p. 110, 56,759; p. 111, 47,736; p. 112, 10,455-L-1; p. 113, T 13,301*; p. 114, 1000-B*; p. 116, 1102-B-26*; p. 117 top, JRS V1 N26*; p. 117 bottom, 45,837-A; p. 118, 4327*; p. 120, 56,963; p. 123, 55,937; p. 124, T 26,537; p. 125, 34,055; p. 126, 34,054-M; p. 127, 56,814; p. 130, 2382*; p. 132, 2372-C-19*; p. 133, 1821-A-2*; p. 134, T 162; p. 135, T 148; p. 136, 41,106-B; p. 137, 2224*; p. 138, 1982-C*; p. 140, 56,747; p. 141, 2189*; p. 142, SI 3946*; p. 144, 56,752; p. 145, 38,582-C; p. 146, 55,297; p. 147, 55,296; p. 148, 2517-A; p. 155, 1280-A*; p. 156, 988-A*; p. 157, 3237-A*; p. 158, 906-B; p. 159, 4251-B; p. 160, 3120-A*; p. 161, 690-B*; p. 162, 1563*; p. 163, 2235-B*; p. 164, 3441*; p. 165, 2793-A*; p. 166, 3438*; p. 167, 52,818*; p. 168, 2575-D-1; p. 170, 2898*; p. 171, 3041*; p. 172 top, 673-A*; p. 172 bottom, 571*; p. 173, 4130-A*; p. 174, 517-B; p. 175, 1140-A*; p. 176, 218-A*; p. 177, 3836-A-1*; p. 178, 55,664; p. 180, 581-B-1*; p.181, 581-B-2*; p. 183, 2909*; p.184, 3200-B-11.

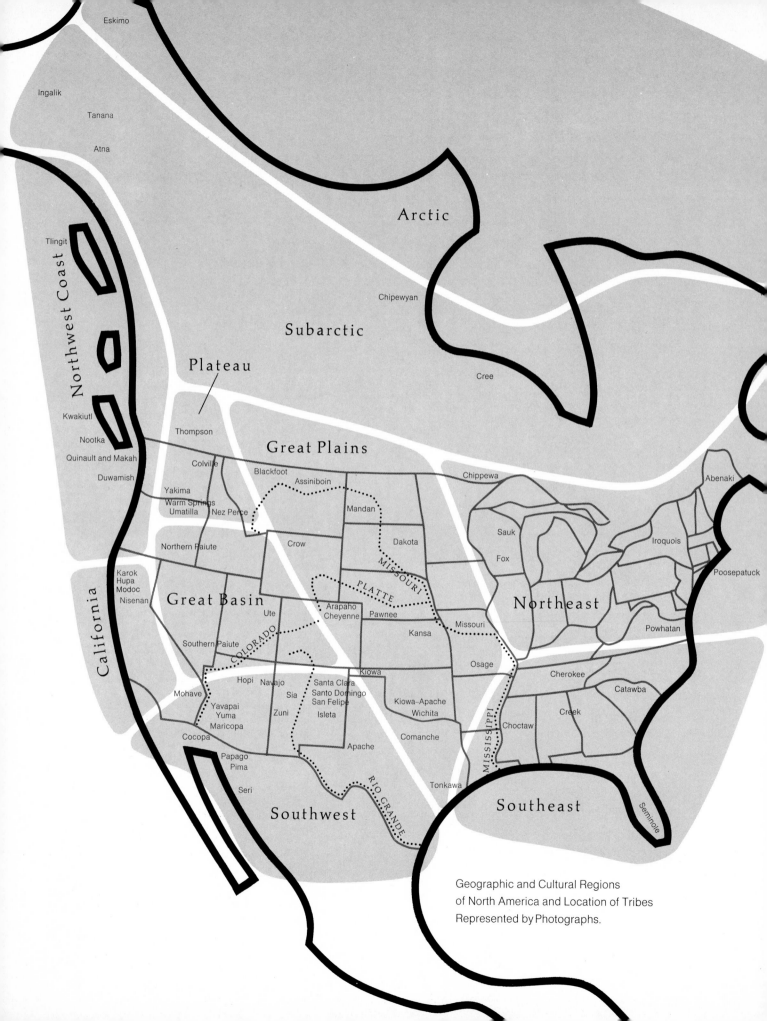

Eskimo

Ingalik

Tanana

Atna

Arctic

Chipewyan

Subarctic

Cree

Tlingit

Northwest Coast

Plateau

Kwakiutl

Nootka

Quinault and Makah

Duwamish

Thompson

Colville

Yakima
Warm Springs
Umatilla

Nez Perce

Northern Paiute

Great Plains

Blackfoot

Assiniboin

Mandan

Dakota

MISSOURI

Chippewa

Abenaki

Sauk

Fox

Iroquois

Poosepatuck

Northeast

Powhatan

Karok
Hupa
Modoc

Nisenan

Great Basin

Ute

Crow

PLATTE

Arapaho
Cheyenne

Pawnee

Kansa

Missouri

California

Southern Paiute

COLORADO

Kiowa

Osage

Cherokee

Catawba

Creek

Mohave

Hopi

Navajo

Sia

Zuni

Santa Clara
Santo Domingo
San Felipe

Isleta

Kiowa–Apache

Wichita

MISSISSIPPI

Choctaw

Yavapai
Yuma
Maricopa

Cocopa

Papago
Pima

Apache

Comanche

Seri

RIO GRANDE

Tonkawa

Southwest

Southeast

Seminole

Geographic and Cultural Regions
of North America and Location of Tribes
Represented by Photographs.